© Alexandra Milton

GILES MILTON is an internationally bestselling author of narrative nonfiction. His books include *Nathaniel's Nutmeg*—serialized by the BBC—and seven other critically acclaimed works of history. Milton's latest title, *The Perfect Corpse,* is his debut thriller. He lives in London with his wife, illustrator Alexandra Milton, and three daughters.

When Hitler Took Cocaine and Lenin Lost His Brain

HISTORY'S UNKNOWN CHAPTERS

Giles Milton

PICADOR

New York

picadorusa.com
twitter.com/picadorusa • facebook.com/picadorusa
picadorbookroom.tumblr.com

Picador® is a U.S. registered trademark and is used by St. Martin's Press under license from Pan Books Limited.

For book club information, please visit facebook.com/picadorbookclub or e-mail marketing@picadorusa.com.

Designed by Michelle McMillian

The Library of Congress Cataloging-in-Publication Data is available upon request.

ISBN 978-1-250-07877-3 (trade paperback)
ISBN 978-1-250-07878-0 (e-book)

Our books may be purchased in bulk for promotional, educational, or business use. Please contact your local bookseller or the Macmillan Corporate and Premium Sales Department at 1-800-221-7945, extension 5442, or by e-mail at MacmillanSpecialMarkets @macmillan.com.

First published in Great Britain under the titles *When Hitler Took Cocaine* and *When Lenin Lost His Brain* by John Murray (Publishers), an Hachette UK company.

First U.S. Edition: January 2016

Contents

Preface   vii

BOOK I: WHEN HITLER TOOK COCAINE

PART I • *I Never Knew That About Hitler*   5

PART II • *Jeez, It's Cold Out There*   19

PART III • *Hell in Japan*   33

PART IV • *Ladies in Disguise*   47

PART V • *Man's Best Friend*   61

PART VI • *Guilty Until Proven Innocent*   73

PART VII • *Big-Time Adventure*   87

PART VIII • *I'm a Celebrity*   101

PART IX • *Not Enough Sex*   117

Further Reading   123

Contents

BOOK II: WHEN LENIN LOST HIS BRAIN

PART I • *When Lenin Lost His Brain*   133

PART II • *Just Bad Luck*   147

PART III • *Not Quite Normal*   163

PART IV • *Mein Führer*   177

PART V • *Get Me Out of Here!*   195

PART VI • *O What a Lovely War!*   205

PART VII • *Dial M for Murder*   219

PART VIII • *The Great Escape*   233

PART IX • *A Painful End*   249

Further Reading   257

Preface

In the summer of 2012, a cache of extraordinary medical documents came to light in America. They included the records of Dr Theodor Morell, personal physician to Adolf Hitler, and notes written by four other doctors who treated the Führer.

At first glance, the documents seemed little more than an historical footnote, one to be added to the mass of existing material about Hitler. But footnotes can often conceal nuggets of gold, and this one opened a wholly unknown chapter of history. The cache revealed that the Führer was being prescribed a heady cocktail of drugs, including cocaine, amphetamines and testosterone. Indeed he was taking up to 80 drugs a day, at the same time as masterminding his attempted conquest of the world.

Much of my working life is spent in the archives, delving through letters and personal papers like those written by Dr Morell. The huge collection housed in Britain's National Archives is incompletely catalogued (the National Archives in Washington DC is somewhat better) and you can never be entirely sure what you will find in any given box of documents.

Days can pass without unearthing anything of interest: I liken it to those metal-detecting treasure-hunters of North Carolina, who scour the Outer Banks in the hope of turning up a Jacobean shilling or signet ring.

Persistence often pays rich dividends, and this book—an idiosyncratic collection of unknown historical chapters—is the result of my own metaphorical metal detecting. Amidst the flotsam and jetsam, I've found (I hope) some glittering gems. There's the lone Japanese soldier still fighting the Second World War in 1974; the British agent-cum-hitman who assassinated Rasputin (as with Dr Morell, this story has only recently come to light); and the tale of the shipwrecked Dutch mariners who ate the last dodo.

Some of the stories are truly eye-stretching. The testimony of Sun Yaoting, the last eunuch of China, is not only painful but extraordinarily poignant. It sheds light on the twilight years of imperial China, when centuries of tradition were swept away in the blink of an eye. Sun Yaoting, alas, was to find himself on the wrong side of history.

I've long believed that historical detail is vitally important when attempting to reconstruct the past. Detail can illuminate events in a way that the broad brushstroke cannot. The obsessive quest on the part of Soviet scientists to find the 'genius' inside Lenin's brain is a case in point. It reveals much about neurological science of the 1920s—then in its infancy—and even more about the Soviet Union's cult of personality, of which this was one of the earliest manifestations.

Many of the stories in this collection are about individuals, often unremarkable individuals, who found themselves caught up in truly extraordinary situations. Some were swept through defining moments of history: Tsutomu Yamaguchi, who survived the atomic bombs at both Hiroshima and Nagasaki, is one of them. Others were unwilling partakers in catastrophe: men like Charles Joughin, who not only survived the *Titanic* disaster, but did so with an amazing story to tell.

Just occasionally, the stories reveal something about ourselves. I've often found myself musing on what *I* would have done if I'd found myself in situations similar to the men and women in this collection. Would I have been as cool under pressure as Walter Harris, the Moroccan correspondent for *The Times*, when captured by murderous Islamic extremists in 1903? I doubt it.

These days, we're unlikely to be exhibited as a human freak, as was Ota Benga, and equally unlikely to be buried alive, as was Augustine Courtauld. But anything can happen to anyone: who knows, you may yet get caught in an adventure that will one day be recognised as a highly prized nugget of history.

Giles Milton, London
January 2016

BOOK I

When Hitler Took Cocaine

Contents

Part I: I Never Knew That About Hitler

1. Hitler's English Girlfriend   7
2. Hitler's American Nephew   11
3. When Hitler Took Cocaine   14

Part II: Jeez, It's Cold Out There

4. A Corpse on Everest   21
5. Drunk on the *Titanic*   26
6. The Man Who Was Buried Alive   29

Part III: Hell in Japan

7. The Long War of Hiroo Onoda   35
8. The Kamikaze Pilot Who Survived   39
9. Surviving Hiroshima and Nagasaki   43

Part IV: Ladies in Disguise

10. Agatha Christie's Greatest Mystery   49

Contents

11. Dressed to Kill   53

12. Mission into Danger   57

Part V: Man's Best Friend

13. The Real War Horse   63

14. Pigeon to the Rescue   66

15. Barking for Victory   70

Part VI: Guilty Until Proven Innocent

16. Angel of Death   75

17. Who Killed Rasputin?   79

18. Till Death Us Do Part   83

Part VII: Big-Time Adventure

19. By Balloon to the North Pole   89

20. Escape from Alcatraz   93

21. A Lonely Trek Through the Andes   96

Part VIII: I'm a Celebrity

22. The First Celebrity Kidnap   103

23. Sir Osman of Hyderabad   107

24. The Very Strange Death of Alfred Loewenstein   111

Part IX: Not Enough Sex

25. The Last Eunuch of China   119

Further Reading   *123*

PART I

I Never Knew That About Hitler

Göring has only got one ball,
Hitler's are so very small,
Himmler's so very similar,
And Goebbels has no balls at all.

THE ORIGINAL WORDS TO *HITLER HAS ONLY
GOT ONE BALL*, CIRCA AUGUST 1939.
ATTRIBUTED TO TOBY O'BRIEN, PUBLICIST FOR
THE BRITISH COUNCIL.

1

Hitler's English Girlfriend

Unity Mitford was a plain-looking woman with bad teeth and a plump belly. But she had never been troubled by her strange looks and knew that she was more likely to catch the man of her dreams by speaking her mind rather than flaunting her body.

In the summer of 1934, she travelled to Munich in the hope of meeting her idol, Adolf Hitler. Although he was Führer of Germany, it was relatively easy to see him in public since he was accustomed to eating at the same cafes and restaurants each day.

When Unity learned that he often had lunch at the Osteria Bavaria, she began eating there as well. She did everything she could to catch his attention. Yet ten months were to pass before Hitler finally invited the persistent English girl to his table. The two of them chatted for half an hour and quickly realized they were soulmates.

'It was the most wonderful and beautiful [day] of my life,' wrote Unity to her father. 'I am so happy that I wouldn't mind a bit, dying. I'd suppose I am the luckiest girl in the world. For me he is the greatest man of all time.'

Her feelings were reciprocated. Hitler was particularly intrigued by Unity's middle name, Valkyrie. And he was fascinated to learn that her grandfather had translated the anti-Semitic works of Houston Stewart Chamberlain, one of his favourite authors.

Hitler began to see more and more of his fair-haired English companion, much to the annoyance of his 'official' girlfriend, Eva Braun. 'She is known as the Valkyrie and looks the part, including her legs,' wrote Braun scornfully in her diary. 'I, the mistress of the greatest man in Germany and the whole world, I sit here waiting while the sun mocks me through the window panes.'

Unity was now introduced to members of Hitler's inner circle. She got along particularly well with the thuggish Julius Streicher, publisher of the vitriolic anti-Semitic newspaper *Der Stürmer*.

When Unity delivered a particularly racist diatribe against the Jews, Streicher asked if he could print it in his paper. Unity was flattered. 'The English have no notion of the Jewish danger,' began her article. 'Our worst Jews work only behind the scenes. We think with joy of the day when we will be able to say England for the English! Out with the Jews! Heil Hitler!' She ended her text with the words: 'Please publish my name in full, I want everyone to know I am a Jew hater.'

Hitler was so pleased with what Unity had written that he awarded her a golden swastika badge as well as a private box at the 1936 Berlin Olympics.

She now became one of the Führer's intimates, visiting him on numerous occasions and constantly expressing her admiration for him. He was no less smitten with her: in 1938, he even offered her an apartment in Munich. Unity had high hopes of replacing Eva Braun in his affections.

By now, her behaviour had aroused the suspicions of the British Secret Service. The head of MI5, Guy Liddell, was particularly alarmed by her closeness to Hitler. He felt that her friendship with him warranted her being put on trial for high treason.

Unity refused to leave Germany, even after Britain's declaration of war on 3 September 1939. Yet she was deeply depressed by what had happened, not least because of the implications it had for her relationship with Hitler.

She took herself to the English Garden in Munich, held to her head the pearl-handled pistol that had been given to her by Hitler and pulled the trigger.

She was badly wounded but, amazingly, survived. Hospitalized in Munich (the bills were paid by Hitler), she was eventually moved to Switzerland. When she had partially recovered, her sister, Deborah, flew to Bern in order to take her home to England.

'We were not prepared for what we found: the person lying in bed was desperately ill. She had lost two stone (28 pounds), was all huge eyes and matted hair, untouched since the bullet went through her skull.'

What happened next remains shrouded in mystery. According to the official account, she was taken to the family home at Swinbrook, Oxfordshire. She learned to walk but never made a full recovery. She eventually died in 1948 as a result of meningitis caused by the bullet in her brain.

But there is also a more intriguing story about her return to England. There are rumours, never confirmed, that she was taken to a private maternity hospital in Oxford. Here, in absolute secrecy, she gave birth to Hitler's love child.

The woman who made the claim, Val Hann, is the niece of the hospital's former manager, Betty Norton. Betty had told the story to her sister, who in turn passed it on to Val.

If true, it would mean that Hitler's child is quite possibly still alive and living somewhere in England.

But the facts will never be known for certain: Betty Norton died long ago and the maternity hospital neglected to register the babies who were born during the war.

2

Hitler's American Nephew

He kept his identity a secret until his dying day. None of his neighbours in Patchogue, Long Island, had any idea that William Stuart Houston was actually born William Hitler. Nor did they know that his uncle had been the Führer of Nazi Germany.

It was not until long after William's death in 1987 that the truth about his identity was made public. But several unanswered questions remain, questions that his sons, three of whom are still alive and living in America, have been unable to answer.

William's story begins in Edwardian Liverpool. Adolf Hitler's half brother, Alois, had moved to the city in 1911. He married his Irish-born lover, Bridgit Dowling, and before long she was pregnant. When baby William was born, the neighbours called him 'Paddy' Hitler.

Alois abandoned his wife and son in 1914 and returned Germany. An entire decade was to pass before he renewed contact with Bridgit. When he did so, he asked her to allow William to travel to Germany.

William made a brief trip to see his father in 1929 and then returned four years later for a much longer stay. By now, he was hoping to profit from his uncle's position as Chancellor of Germany.

Hitler initially got him a temporary job in a bank. Some time later, he wangled him employment in an automobile factory, a job that William disliked intensely. He repeatedly begged his uncle for a better job, but Hitler refused to help his nephew any further. Indeed, William eventually found himself suspended from his work on Hitler's orders. He was accused of trying to sell cars for his own profit.

William continued to see Hitler occasionally, but Adolf was no longer the friendly uncle of old. 'I shall never forget the last time he sent for me,' wrote William. 'He was in a brutal temper when I arrived. Walking back and forth, brandishing his horse-hide whip . . . he shouted insults at my head as if he were delivering a political oration. His vengeful brutality on that day made me fear for my physical safety.'

William realized it was time to leave Germany. In February 1939, he sailed for the United States.

As war began, William began a lecture tour of the USA, denouncing his Führer-uncle for his extravagant lifestyle. 'Far from scorning lavish display,' he told his audiences, 'he has surrounded himself with luxury more extravagant than any Kaiser ever enjoyed. To decorate his new chancellery in Berlin, every museum in Germany was plundered for priceless carpets, tapestries, paintings.'

When America joined the war, William wrote to President Roosevelt asking for permission to join the US Army. The letter was sent to the FBI, who cleared him for service. According to one paper, his recruiting officer said: 'Glad to see you Hitler. My name's Hess.'

At the war's end, William set up a medical laboratory that analysed blood samples for hospitals. As the Nuremberg Trials got under way, he tried to make a complete break with his Hitler past. He changed his name to William Stuart Houston and settled with his wife in Long Island. They would eventually have four sons, three of whom remain alive to this day.

William died in 1987 and was buried in anonymity in the same grave as his mother. And there the story might have ended, were it not for an American journalist named David Gardner who began investigating the Hitler family. He eventually stumbled across the strange story of William Hitler, and discovered that members of the Hitler clan were alive and well and living in America.

The family insist that William hated Hitler until his dying day and they proudly point to his unblemished war record, fighting against Nazi Germany.

Yet two enigmas remain. Why did William Hitler chose as his new name Stuart Houston, one that is strikingly close to the name of Adolf Hitler's favourite anti-Semitic author, Houston Stewart Chamberlain?

And why did William give his eldest son, Alexander, the middle name Adolf?

3

When Hitler Took Cocaine

The injections began shortly after breakfast. As soon as Adolf Hitler had finished his bowl of oatmeal and linseed oil he would summon his personal physician, Theodor Morell.

The doctor would roll up his patient's sleeve in order to inject an extraordinary cocktail of drugs, many of which are these days classed as dangerous, addictive and illegal.

Every day for more than nine years, Dr Morell administered amphetamines, barbiturates and opiates in such quantities that he became known as the Reichsmaster of Injections. Some in Hitler's inner circle wondered if he wasn't trying to kill the Führer.

But Theodor Morell was far too devoted to Hitler to murder him. A grossly obese quack doctor with acrid halitosis and appalling body odour, he had first met the Führer at a party at the Berghof.

Hitler had long suffered from ill health, including stomach

cramps, diarrhoea and such chronic flatulence than he had to leave the table after each meal in order to expel vast quantities of wind.

His condition was aggravated by his unconventional diet. He had forsaken meat in 1931 after comparing eating ham to eating a human corpse. Henceforth, he ate large quantities of watery vegetables, pureed or mashed to a pulp. Dr Morell watched the Führer eat one such meal and then studied the consequences. 'Constipations and colossal flatulence occurred on a scale I have seldom encountered before,' he wrote. He assured Hitler he had miracle drugs that could cure all of his problems.

He began by administering little black tablets called Dr Küster's Anti-Gas pills. Hitler took sixteen a day, apparently unaware that they contained quantities of strychnine. Although they alleviated his wind – temporarily – they almost certainly triggered the attention lapses and sallow skin that were to mark his final years.

Morell next prescribed a type of hydrolysed E. coli bacteria called Mutaflor, which seemed to further stabilize the Führer's bowel problems. Indeed Hitler was so pleased with the doctor's work that he invited him to join the inner circle of Nazi elite. Henceforth, Morell was never far from his side.

Along with his stomach cramps, Hitler also suffered from morning grogginess. To alleviate this, Morell injected him with a watery fluid that he concocted from a powder kept in gold-foil packets. He never revealed the active ingredient in this medicine, called Vitamultin, but it worked wonders on every occasion it was administered. Within a few minutes, Hitler would arise from his couch invigorated and full of energy.

Ernst-Günther Schenck, an SS doctor, grew suspicious of

Dr Morell's miracle cures and managed to acquire one of the packets. When tested in a laboratory, it was found to be amphetamine.

Hitler was untroubled by what he was given, just so long as the drugs worked. It was not long before he became so dependent on Morell's 'cures' that he placed all his health problems entirely in the doctor's hands, with disastrous long-term consequences. He directed the invasion of Soviet Russia while being pumped with as many as eighty different drugs, including testosterone, opiates, sedatives and laxatives. According to the doctor's medical notebooks, he also administered barbiturates, morphine, bull semen and probiotics.

The most surprising drug that Dr Morell prescribed to the Führer was cocaine. This was occasionally used for medical ailments in 1930s Germany, but always in extremely low dosages and at a concentration of less than one per cent. Morell began administering cocaine to the Führer by means of eye-drops. Aware that Hitler expected to feel better after taking his drugs, he put ten times the amount of cocaine into the drops. Such a concentrated dose may well have triggered the psychotic behaviour that Hitler was to experience in his later years.

The Führer found cocaine extremely efficacious. According to a cache of medical documents that came to light in America in 2012 (including a forty-seven-page report written by Morell and other doctors who attended the Führer), Hitler soon began to 'crave' the drug. It was a clear sign that he was developing a serious addiction. As well as the eye-drops, he now began to snort powdered cocaine 'to clear his sinuses and soothe his throat'.

Cocaine may have induced a feeling of well-being but it did nothing to boost the Führer's lack of sexual drive. To overcome this embarrassing condition, Morell began giving him virility injections. These contained extracts from the prostate glands of young bulls. Morell also prescribed a medicine called Testoviron, a medication derived from testosterone. Hitler would have himself injected before spending the night with Eva Braun.

The long-term effect of taking such drugs, particularly amphetamines, led to increasingly erratic behaviour. The most visible manifestation of this came at a meeting between Hitler and Mussolini in northern Italy. As Hitler tried to persuade his Italian counterpart not to change sides in the war, he became wildly hysterical. According to Third Reich historian Richard Evans: 'We can be pretty sure Morell gave some tablets to Hitler when he went to see Mussolini . . . [he was] completely hyper in every way, talking, gabbling, clearly on speed.'

As the war drew to a close, Hitler was in very poor health. Dependent on drugs, his arms were so punctured with hypodermic marks that Eva Braun accused Morell of being an 'injection quack'. He had turned Hitler into an addict. Yet the doctor continued to hero-worship his beloved Führer and remained with him in his Berlin bunker until almost the end.

Dr Morell was captured by the Americans soon after the fall of the Third Reich and interrogated for more than two years. One of the officers who questioned him was disgusted by his lack of personal hygiene.

Morell was never charged with war crimes and he died of a stroke in 1948, shortly after his release from prison. He left behind a cache of medical notebooks that reveal the extraordinary drug addiction of his favourite patient.

It is ironic that the man charged with restoring Hitler to good health probably did more than anyone else to contribute to his decline.

PART II

Jeez, It's Cold Out There

Insurance claims for pets on the *Titanic*
who drowned in icy seawater

ROBERT W. DANIEL

One pedigree French bulldog named
Gamin de Pycombe: $750

WILLIAM CARTER

One King Charles Spaniel and one
Airdale Terrier: $300

ELLA HOLMES WHITE

Four roosters and hens: $207.87

HARRY ANDERSON

One chow-chow: $50

4

A Corpse on Everest

The corpse was frozen and bleached by the sun. It lay face down in the snow, fully extended and pointing uphill. The upper body was welded to the scree with ice. The arms, still muscular, were outstretched above the head.

Mountaineer George Mallory had last been sighted on 8 June 1924, when he and Andrew Irvine went missing while attempting to become the first men to reach the summit of Everest. Whether or not they achieved this goal has been the subject of intense speculation for ninety years.

In the spring of 1999, an American named Eric Simonson set up the Mallory and Irvine Research Expedition. Five experienced mountaineers were sent high onto Everest with the aim of finding the bodies of one or both climbers.

They had a few clues to help them in their search. In 1975, a Chinese climber named Wang Hung-bao had stumbled across 'an English dead' at 26,570 feet (8,100 metres). Wang reported the find to his climbing partner shortly before being swept away by an avalanche. The precise location of the 'English dead' was never fixed.

Eric Simonson's five-strong team of experienced mountaineers were undeterred. Conrad Anker, Dave Hahn, Jake Norton, Andy Politz, and Tap Richards were determined to succeed, even though the odds were stacked against them.

Their search was concentrated on a wide snow-terrace the size of twelve football pitches. Tilted at a crazy angle, the terrace lay above 26,000 feet. The men knew that if they lost their balance, the thirty degree slope would carry them down a 7,000-foot drop to the Rongbuk Glacier.

On 1 May, Conrad Anker was combing the slope when he raised a cry. He had spotted a corpse, white as alabaster, sticking out of the ice. The rest of the team made their way towards him and began chipping the corpse from its frozen resting place. As they dug, they studied the body with care. The tibia and fibula of the right leg were broken, the right elbow was dislocated and the right side also badly damaged. The climbing rope had wrapped itself tightly around the ribcage.

It didn't take long to identify the body. When Tap Richards looked inside the clothing, he found a name-tag: *G Mallory*.

'Maybe it was the altitude and the fact that we'd all put aside our oxygen gear,' said Dave Hahn, 'but it took a while for reality to sink in. We were in the presence of George Mallory himself.'

The question that remained unanswered was whether or not Mallory and Irvine had made it to the summit. Did they die on their way up? Or on their way down?

The team hoped they might find Mallory's camera: experts at Kodak had said that the film, though old, might yet be developed. But when the men reached inside the pouch around

Mallory's neck, they found only a metal tin of stock cubes: 'Brand & Co. Savoury Meat Lozenges'.

There was other evidence as well: a brass altimeter, a pocket-knife, a monogrammed handkerchief and a pair of undamaged sun goggles in an inside pocket.

The goggles were potentially an important clue as to what had happened on that day in 1924. Just a few days before his attempt on the summit, Mallory's second climbing partner, Edward Norton, had suffered serious snow-blindness because he'd neglected to wear his goggles.

Mallory would not have dispensed with his goggles if climbing in daylight. The fact they were in his pocket suggested that the two men had completed their push for the summit in sunlight and were making their descent after dark.

No less interesting was an envelope found on Mallory's body. It was covered in numbers: pressure readings of the oxygen bottles they were carrying. It had long been believed that the climbers didn't have enough oxygen to get them to the summit. But the numbers showed that the two climbers were carrying five, perhaps six canisters – more than enough to get to the top of the mountain.

More tantalizing was an item that the searchers had expected to find on Mallory's body. He was known to have been carrying a photograph of his wife, Ruth, which he had vowed to leave on the summit. The photo was nowhere to be found, even though his wallet and other papers were intact.

The men who found Mallory were able to piece together a plausible scenario as to what happened on the fateful evening of his death. It is a story of adventure and tragic error – one that ultimately led to his doom.

It is late in the evening on 8 June, long after twilight, and the two climbers are still high on the mountain. Exhausted and with failing oxygen supplies, they are desperate to reach safety. As they cross a notoriously treacherous layer of marble and phyllite known as the 'Yellow Band', one of the two climbers slips.

It may well have been Mallory. If so, his fall is halted by the rope, which dashes him into a rocky outcrop. His ribs are instantly broken and his elbow is dislocated. But he is held there by the rope, dangling in a void.

And then, unexpectedly, the rope snaps and he plunges through the darkness. He lands on a steep shelf of snow, snapping his tibia and fibula. But still he doesn't stop. Gravity drags him down the North Face at tremendous speed.

He's terrified and in appalling pain, but still conscious and trying to save himself. In desperation, he clutches at frozen scree, digging his fingers into the ice. Faster and faster he slides until his forehead smashes into a jagged outcrop of rock. It punctures a hole in his head.

He comes to a standstill at the same time as he loses consciousness. Pain and hypothermia rapidly take over. Within minutes, George Mallory is dead.

Irvine, meanwhile, has almost certainly met with a similar fate. He's fallen, seriously injured, and is also suffering from hypothermia. Within a few minutes of Mallory's death he, too, has succumbed to the cold.

But did they make it to the summit? Were they the first to climb Everest? It's a question that Eric Simonson's team was unable to answer with absolute certainty. The discovery of Mallory's body was a remarkable find, but the riddle is likely to remain unsolved unless or until the camera is found.

One person alone has felt able to say whether or not Mallory and Irvine deserve the title of 'conquerors of Everest'. Mallory's son, John, was just three years old when he lost his father. To him, George Mallory's failure to return home provided all the answers he needed. 'To me,' he said, 'the only way you achieve a summit is to come back alive. The job is only half done if you don't get down again.'

5

Drunk on the *Titanic*

It was 14 April 1912. Charles Joughin had finally fallen asleep after a hard day's work in the ship's kitchens. Suddenly, he was woken by a tremendous jolt. He felt the vessel shudder violently beneath him. Then, after a momentary pause, it continued moving forward.

Joughin was puzzled but not unduly alarmed. He knew that icebergs had been sighted in the water; he also knew that Captain Edward Smith had ordered a change of course, steering the *Titanic* onto a more southerly route in order to avoid potential disaster. Assuming that the danger had passed, Joughin tried to return to sleep. But at about 11.35 p.m., just a few minutes after the jolt, he was summoned to the bridge. Here, he was given some most unwelcome information.

Captain Smith had sent an inspection team below decks to see if anything was wrong. The men had returned with the terrible news that the ship had struck an iceberg and that the force of the blow had seriously buckled the hull. Rivets had been forced out over a length of some ninety metres and seawater was now gushing into the ship at a tremendous rate.

This news might have been expected to cause panic. Yet it didn't. Most people believed the *Titanic* to be unsinkable. She had watertight compartments that could be closed in the event of disaster. This meant that even the most serious damage to the ship's hull could be contained.

But now, in this moment of crisis, these watertight compartments were revealed to have a catastrophic design flaw. As they filled with water, so they weighed down the ship's bow, allowing water to pour into other areas of the stricken vessel. A fourth, fifth and then a sixth compartment had already filled with water: it became obvious to Captain Smith that the *Titanic* was inevitably doomed to sink.

Joughin, the *Titanic*'s chief baker, now swung into action. He aroused his fellow chefs from their beds and began to gather all the loaves of bread they could find. They then rushed back on deck and put four loaves into each lifeboat. They already knew that there were not enough boats for all the passengers. The *Titanic* had 2,223 people on board, yet there were only enough lifeboats for 1,178 people.

Charles Joughin realized that he, as a member of crew, would not be given a place in a lifeboat. As the ship began listing at an alarming angle, he decided to drink himself into oblivion. He descended into his cabin, downed a huge quantity of whisky (according to one account he finished off two bottles). He then returned to the deck and, with drunken energy, began pushing women into the lifeboats.

Once this was done, he staggered along the heavily listing promenade deck, wondering how long it would take for the ship to sink. He threw overboard some fifty deckchairs, along with other seats and cushions, in the hope that people in the water might be able to use them as rafts.

It was not long before he, too, found himself in the freezing Atlantic. 'I got onto the starboard side of the poop,' he later recalled, 'and found myself in the water. I do not believe my head went under the water at all. I thought I saw some wreckage.'

He swam towards this, not feeling the cold on account of all the whisky he had drunk, 'and found a collapsible boat B with Lightoller and about twenty-five men on it'.

There was no room for Joughin. 'I tried to get on,' he said, 'but was pushed off, but I hung around. I got around to the opposite side and cook Maynard, who recognized me, helped me and held on to me.'

By this time, it was a miracle Joughin was still alive. The water temperature was two degrees below freezing. Most passengers and crew who had jumped into the water had died of hypothermia within fifteen minutes.

Yet Joughin was to remain in the water for a further four hours before he was finally pulled aboard a lifeboat that came alongside collapsible boat B. Along with the other survivors, he was eventually rescued by the *RMS Carpathia*, which arrived at the wreck site at 4.10 a.m.

Joughin believed that his extraordinary survival was due to the vast quantity of whisky he had drunk. Not so fortunate were 1,517 of his fellow crew and passengers. They died in the water, sober and cold.

The *Titanic* catastrophe was not Joughin's last shipwreck. He was on board the *SS Oregon* when she sank in Boston Harbour. He survived that disaster as well, although it is not known if he had once again fortified himself with a bottle or two of whisky.

6

The Man Who Was Buried Alive

Augustine Courtauld, a young London stockbroker, was bored with his job. He was bored with the paperwork. He was bored with his colleagues. He was desperate to do something more exciting with his life.

In 1930, he learned that volunteers were being recruited for an expedition to conduct weather observations at Icecap Station, a purpose-built post on the Greenland ice sheet. It was 2,600 metres above sea level and 112 miles west of the expedition's main base. And it was very, very cold.

Weather data for Arctic Greenland was desperately needed. The quickest air route from Europe to North America was over the ice sheet, but no one knew what the weather was like, especially in the winter months. Augustine Courtauld went to find out.

He travelled from the coast with a party whose task was to supply the weather station with enough food and fuel for two men. 'But atrocious weather had so slowed down the journey that most of the food intended for the station was eaten on the way there. It looked as if the place would have to be closed down.' So wrote one of the men accompanying the supply party.

Courtauld thought that it would be a shame to abandon the expedition simply because there was not enough food. 'I worked out that I could last out alone for five months,' he later wrote. 'As I had frostbite in my toes, I had no wish to make the journey back. So I decided to stay on my own and keep the station going.'

Frostbitten toes is an eccentric reason for choosing to stay on the Greenland ice sheet in midwinter, but to Courtauld it had a certain logic. He could at least put his feet up for a few months.

Soon after settling into his new home it began to snow. Hard. His small tent was buried by drifting snow until only the tip of the ventilator pipe poked above the surface. Soon he was completely snowed in and effectively buried alive.

His supplies of food and fuel were soon depleted and he had no communication with the outside world. But he remained confident that a rescue team would eventually find him.

'As each month passed without relief, I felt more and more certain of its arrival,' he later wrote. 'By the time I was snowed in I had no doubts on the matter, which was a great comfort to my mind. I will not attempt any explanation of this, but leave it as a fact, which was very clear to me during that time, that while powerless to help myself, some outer force was in action on my side and I wasn't fated to leave my bones on the Greenland ice cap.'

Never once did he despair. Instead, he dreamed of roaring fires and his wife, Mollie, singing to him. He also prayed that Gino Watkins, with whom he had travelled to the base, would soon be coming to the rescue.

'I began to feel complete confidence,' he wrote. 'I knew that even if Gino was having to wait for better weather, he wouldn't let me down. I began to realize that I should not be left to die. I came to know that I was held by Everlasting Arms.'

On 5 May, exactly five months after he was left alone, the Primus gave its last gasp. 'Very soon, there was a noise like a football match overhead. They had come! A hole of brilliant daylight appeared in the roof. There was Gino's voice saying: 'Put these on.' He handed me a pair of snow-glasses. How different it was from the last time I had seen the outside world! It was May and now dazzling sunshine. I had not realized it would be like this.

'They lost no time in pulling me out and I found I was quite all right. My legs were a bit weak. We set out for home next day. I rode on a sledge the whole way, reading *The Count of Monte Cristo*. Conditions were good and we completed the journey in five days. It had taken us six weeks on the way up.'

Courtauld declined to return to his former life as a stockbroker after his Greenland experience. Instead, he undertook an extraordinary six-hundred-mile journey down the unmapped Greenland coastline, travelling in an eighteen-foot open whaleboat.

It was more interesting than sitting behind a desk in London.

PART III

Hell in Japan

Just before the collision it is essential that you do not shut your eyes for a moment so as not to miss the target. Many have crashed into the targets with wide-open eyes. They will tell you what fun they had.

INSTRUCTIONS TO SECOND WORLD WAR
KAMIKAZE PILOTS:
KAMIKAZE, BY ALBERT AXELL AND HIDEAKI KASE

7

The Long War of Hiroo Onoda

His home was a dense area of rainforest and he lived on the wild coconuts that grew in abundance. His principal enemy was the army of mosquitoes that arrived with each new shower of rain. But for Hiroo Onoda, there was another enemy, one that remained elusive.

Unaware that the Second World War had ended twenty-nine years earlier, he was still fighting a lonely guerrilla war in the jungles of the Philippines.

The Americans had landed on Lubang Island in February 1945. Six months later, the Second World War had come to an end. Yet Hiroo Onoda and his small band of men had never received any orders to lay down their weapons. Rather, they'd been instructed to fight to the bitter end. Onoda was still carrying out these orders in 1974: his story is one of courage, farce and loyalty gone mad.

Hiroo Onoda was born to be a soldier. He had enlisted in the Imperial Japanese Army at the age of twenty, receiving training in intelligence and guerrilla warfare. In December 1944, he and a small group of elite soldiers were sent to Lubang Island in the Philippines.

Their mission was to destroy the island's little airstrip and port facilities. They were prohibited, under any circumstances, from surrendering or committing suicide. 'You are absolutely forbidden to die by your own hand', read Onoda's military order. 'So long as you have one soldier, you are to continue to lead him. You may have to live on coconuts. If that's the case, live on coconuts! Under no circumstances are you [to] give up your life voluntarily.'

Onoda was unsuccessful in destroying Lubang's landing facilities, enabling American and Philippine forces to capture the island in February 1945. Most of the Japanese soldiers were either taken prisoner or killed. But Onoda and three others fled to the hills, from where they vowed to continue the fight.

Lubang Island was small: sixteen miles long and just six miles wide. Yet it was covered in dense forest and the four Japanese soldiers found it easy to remain in hiding. They spent their time conducting guerrilla activities, killing at least thirty Filipinos in one attack and clashing with the police on several other occasions.

In October 1945, the men stumbled across a leaflet that read: 'The war ended on August 15. Come down from the mountains.' Onoda did not believe it: he was convinced it was Allied propaganda.

A couple of months later, the men found a second leaflet that had been dropped from the air. It was a surrender order issued by General Tomoyuki Yamashita, Commander of the Fourteenth Army. Once again, Onoda and his men did not believe it to be genuine and vowed to continue Japanese resistance.

Four long years passed and still the little band were living in the forest. But by now, one of the four – Yuichi Akatsu – had

had enough. He abandoned his comrades, surrendered to the Filipino army and returned to Japan. He informed the army that three of his comrades still believed the war to be ongoing.

Another two years passed before family photographs and letters were dropped into the forest on Lubang Island. Onoda found the parcels but was convinced it was all part of an elaborate trick. He and his two companions remained determined to continue fighting until the bitter end. They had little equipment and almost no provisions. They survived by eating coconuts and bananas and occasionally killing a cow.

Their living conditions were abominable. There was tropical heat, constant rain and infestations of rats. All the while they slept in makeshift huts made from branches.

Years rolled into decades and the men began to feel the effects of age. One of Onoda's comrades was killed by local Filipinos in 1954. Another lived for a further eighteen years before being shot in October 1972. He and Onoda had been engaged in a guerrilla raid on Lubang's food supplies when they got caught in a shoot-out.

Onoda was now alone, the last Japanese soldier still fighting the Second World War, a conflict that had ended twenty-seven years earlier. By now his struggle had become a lonely one, yet he refused to lay down his arms. He was still conducting guerrilla raids in the spring of 1974, when a travelling Japanese student, Noria Suzuki, managed to track him down and make contact with him.

Suzuki broke the news that the war had ended a long time previously. Onoda refused to believe it. He told Suzuki he would never surrender until he received specific orders to that effect from his superior officer.

Only now did the Japanese government get involved in trying

to bring Onoda's war to an end. They managed to locate his previous commanding officer, Major Taniguchi, who was fortunately still alive. The major was flown to Lubang Island in order to tell Onoda in person to lay down his weapons.

He was finally successful on 9 March 1974. 'Japan,' he said to Onoda, 'had lost the war and all combat activity was to cease immediately.'

Onoda was officially relieved from military duties and told to hand over his rifle, ammunition and hand grenades. He was both stunned and horrified by what Major Taniguchi had told him. 'We really lost the war!' were his first words. 'How could they [the Japanese army] have been so sloppy?'

When he returned to Japan, he was feted as a national hero. But Onoda disliked the attention and found Japan a mere shadow of the noble imperial country he had served for so many years. He felt sure that if more soldiers had been prepared to fight to the bitter end, just like him, then Japan might have won the war.

8

The Kamikaze Pilot Who Survived

They were almost the same age – two young Japanese pilots who had joined the elite Tokkotai Special Attack Squadron. Now they had volunteered their services as kamikaze fighters prepared to sacrifice their lives for Japan.

It was spring 1945. Shigeyoshi Hamazono and Kiyoshi Ogawa were about to embark on their final mission, a devastating attack on American warships based in the waters around Okinawa.

Operation Kikusui was planned as a rolling wave of kamikaze attacks involving more than 1,500 planes. But the mission did not go entirely to plan, as Shigeyoshi Hamazono was soon to discover.

Hamazono had volunteered to serve in the Japanese military after the bombing of Pearl Harbour in December 1941. His mother was appalled: 'She wrote me a letter with the only words she could manage: "Don't be defeated. Don't die."' This injunction seemed a forlorn one, for Hamazono was selected to take part in Operation Kikusui.

Service in the Special Attack Squadrons was supposed to be entirely voluntary. The pilots in Hamazono's group had previously been given a recruitment form and told to mark it with a circle if they volunteered, or a cross if they declined.

'Three men marked a cross,' recalled Hamazono, 'and they were forced to go anyway. I felt hatred towards those officers who made them go like that.'

Hamazono himself was given little choice when nominated for Operation Kikusui. He was called by the commander and told that he'd been selected for the following day's attack.

'As a military pilot, there was no way to say no . . . It was my duty. That night, all I thought about was my mission.'

He had already survived one abortive suicide mission: his plane had developed technical failure and he had been forced to return to base. Now he was despatched on what was supposed to be his final attack. He climbed into his Mitsubishi Zero fighter, knowing that he would never see his family again.

Before heading out towards the US fleet, he flew over his hometown and dropped a *hachimaki* headband with the words: 'Hope you are well, goodbye'. It was a symbolic farewell.

His comrade-in-arms, Kiyoshi Ogawa, was rather more enthusiastic. He had been desperate to join the kamikaze squadron and was looking forward to the attack. He had no second thoughts as he climbed into his plane for his final mission.

Ogawa was one of the first to approach the American ships. As he did so, his plane came under sustained anti-aircraft fire. Undaunted, he kept flying directly towards his target, the American aircraft carrier *USS Bunker Hill*. When he was overhead, he pushed his plane into a steep dive, simultaneously dropping a 550lb bomb.

The warhead penetrated *Bunker Hill*'s flight deck and exploded, setting fire to fuel. The flames spread to the refuelled planes on deck, which promptly exploded. Ogawa just had time to see the carnage he had caused before delivering his coup de grâce, crashing the plane into the ship's burning control tower.

There was utter devastation on board. The explosion killed many of *Bunker Hill*'s pilots waiting inside the 'ready room', burning the oxygen and asphyxiating the men.

Hamazono was also intent on hitting his target ship. But as he neared the American fleet, he noticed that a squadron of US fighters had been scrambled to meet him.

There followed a dangerous thirty-five-minute dogfight, with Hamazono dodging the American bullets while at the same time trying to identify his target far below. 'At the end of the dogfight, I could see them coming at me again from a long way off. I was certain that I would be killed in a matter of seconds. But as they got closer, they banked and flew off. I still can't work out why they did that.'

Hamazono was by now flying an aircraft riddled with holes. He also had severe cuts and burns to both his face and hands. As darkness was approaching, he decided to limp back to the Japanese mainland rather than press on with his attack. 'I was burned all over and only had five of my teeth left.' His mission was at an end.

Hamazono was not selected for another kamikaze raid. The war was almost over and he had lost all desire to die inside his plane.

For many years afterwards, he and the handful of other surviving kamikaze pilots had to live with the stigma of having survived a mission that ought to have claimed their lives.

'They used to tell us that the last words of the pilots were: "Long Live the Emperor!"' says Hamazono. 'But I am sure that was a lie. They cried out what I would have cried. They called for their mothers.'

9

Surviving Hiroshima and Nagasaki

He was travelling across Hiroshima on a public tram when he heard the droning sound of an aircraft engine in the skies above.

Tsutomu Yamaguchi thought nothing of it. After all, it was wartime and planes were forever passing above the city. He was unaware that the engines belonged to the US bomber *Enola Gay*, and that it was just seconds away from dropping a thirteen kiloton uranium atomic bomb on the city.

As the plane approached its target at 8.15 a.m. on 6 August 1945, Yamaguchi had just stepped off the tram. He glanced at the sky and noticed a bomber passing overheard. He also saw two small parachutes. And then, quite without warning, all hell broke loose.

'[There was] a great flash in the sky and I was blown over.' The massive nuclear warhead had exploded less than three kilometres from the spot where he was standing.

The bomb was detonated at six hundred metres above Hiroshima. As Yamaguchi swung his gaze upwards, he saw a vast mushroom-shaped pillar of fire rising high into the sky. Seconds later, he passed out. The blast caused his eardrums to rupture and the flash of light left him temporarily blinded.

The heat of the explosion was such that it left him with serious burns over the left side of his body. When he eventually regained consciousness, he crawled to a shelter and tried to make sense of what had happened. Fortunately, he stumbled across three colleagues, who had also survived. All were young engineers working for the shipbuilder Mitsubishi Heavy Industries. They had been unlucky enough to be sent to Hiroshima on the very day of the bombing.

They spent the night together in an air-raid shelter, nursing their burns and wounds. Then, on the following morning, they ventured out of their shelter and picked their way through the charred and molten ruins. As they went to the nearest functioning railway station they passed piles of burnt and dying bodies. Their aim was to catch one of the few working trains back to their hometown of Nagasaki, some 200 miles away.

Yamaguchi was in a poor state and went to have his wounds bandaged as soon as he reached Nagasaki. But by 9 August, after just two days of convalescence, he felt well enough to struggle into work.

His boss and his co-workers listened in horrified amazement as he described the unbelievable destruction that a single bomb had managed to cause. He told them how the explosion had melted metal and evaporated entire parts of the city. His boss, Sam, simply didn't believe him.

'You're an engineer,' he barked. 'Calculate it. How could one bomb destroy a whole city?'

At the exact moment he said these words – 11.02 a.m. – there was a blinding white flash that penetrated to the heart of the room. Yamaguchi's tender skin was once again pricked with heat and he crashed to the ground. 'I thought that the mushroom cloud followed me from Hiroshima,' he said later.

The US Air Force had dropped their second nuclear warhead – Fat Man – named after Winston Churchill. It was much larger than the Hiroshima device, a twenty-five kiloton plutonium bomb that exploded in the bowl of the valley where Nagasaki is situated.

The destruction was more confined but even more intense than at Hiroshima. Some 74,000 were killed and a similar number injured.

Yamaguchi, his wife and his baby son miraculously survived and spent much of the following week in an air-raid shelter near what was left of their home. Five days later, they heard the news that Emperor Hirohito had announced Japan's surrender.

Yamaguchi's survival of both nuclear explosions was little short of miraculous. Yet it was later discovered that he was one of 160 people known to have lived through both bombings.

In 1957, he was recognized as a *hibakusha* or 'explosion affected person'. But it was not until 2009 that he was officially allowed to describe himself as an *eniijuu hibakusha* or double bomb survivor.

The effects of the double bombings left its scars, both mental and physical. Yamaguchi lost the hearing in his left ear as a result of the Hiroshima explosion. He also lost his hair temporarily. His daughter would later recall that he was swathed in bandages until she reached the age of twelve.

Yamaguchi became an outspoken opponent of nuclear weapons until he was well advanced in years, at which point he began to suffer from the long-term effects of the exposure to radiation. His wife developed liver and kidney cancer in 2008 and died soon after. Yamaguchi himself developed acute leukaemia and died in 2010 at the age of ninety-three. His longevity was extraordinary, as he knew only too well. He viewed his long life as a 'path planted by God'.

'It was my destiny that I experienced this twice and I am still alive to convey what happened,' he said towards the end of his life.

PART IV

Ladies in Disguise

In final effect my outfit might deceive any eye; it revealed a thick-set and plump figure, finished by a somewhat small head and a boyish face.

DOROTHY LAWRENCE ADMIRES HER DISGUISE AS A
FIRST WORLD WAR SOLDIER

10

Agatha Christie's Greatest Mystery

At shortly after 9.30 p.m. on Friday 3 December 1926, Agatha Christie got up from her armchair and climbed the stairs of her Berkshire home. She kissed her sleeping daughter, Rosalind, aged seven, goodnight and made her way back downstairs again. Then she climbed into her Morris Cowley and drove off into the night. She would not be seen again for eleven days.

Her disappearance would spark one of the largest manhunts ever mounted. Agatha Christie was already a famous writer and more than one thousand policemen were assigned to the case, along with hundreds of civilians. For the first time, aeroplanes were also involved in the search.

The Home Secretary, William Joynson-Hicks, urged the police to make faster progress in finding her. Two of Britain's most famous crime writers, Sir Arthur Conan Doyle, creator of Sherlock Holmes, and Dorothy L. Sayers, author of the Lord Peter Wimsey series, were drawn into the search. Their specialist knowledge, it was hoped, would help find the missing writer.

It didn't take long for the police to locate her car. It was found abandoned on a steep slope at Newlands Corner near Guildford. But there was no sign of Agatha Christie herself and nor was there any evidence that she'd been involved in an accident.

As the first day of investigations progressed into the second and third – and there was still no sign of her – speculation began to mount. The press had a field day, inventing ever more lurid theories as to what might have happened.

It was the perfect tabloid story, with all the elements of an Agatha Christie whodunnit. Close to the scene of the car accident was a natural spring known as the Silent Pool, where two young children were reputed to have died. Some journalists ventured to suggest that the novelist had deliberately drowned herself.

Yet her body was nowhere to be found and suicide seemed unlikely, for her professional life had never looked so optimistic. Her sixth novel, *The Murder of Roger Ackroyd*, was selling well and she was already a household name.

Some said the incident was nothing more than a publicity stunt, a clever ruse to promote her new book. Others hinted at a far more sinister turn of events. There were rumours that she'd been murdered by her husband, Archie Christie, a former First World War pilot and serial philanderer. He was known to have a mistress.

Arthur Conan Doyle, a keen occultist, tried using paranormal powers to solve the mystery. He took one of Christie's gloves to a celebrated medium in the hope that it would provide answers. It did not.

Dorothy Sayers visited the scene of the writer's disappearance to search for possible clues. This proved no less futile.

By the second week of the search, the news had spread around the world. It even made the front page of the *New York Times*.

Not until 14 December, fully eleven days after she disappeared, was Agatha Christie finally located. She was found safe and well in a hotel in Harrogate, but in circumstances so strange that they raised more questions than they solved. Christie herself was unable to provide any clues to what had happened. She remembered nothing. It was left to the police to piece together what might have taken place.

They came to the conclusion that Agatha Christie had left home and travelled to London, crashing her car en route. She had then boarded a train to Harrogate. On arriving at the spa town, she checked into the Swan Hydro – now the Old Swan Hotel – with almost no luggage. Bizarrely, she used the assumed name of Theresa Neele, her husband's mistress.

Harrogate was the height of elegance in the 1920s and filled with fashionable young things. Agatha Christie did nothing to arouse suspicions as she joined in with the balls, dances and Palm Court entertainment. She was eventually recognized by one of the hotel's banjo players, Bob Tappin, who alerted the police. They tipped off her husband, Colonel Christie, who came to collect Agatha immediately.

But his wife was in no hurry to leave. Indeed, she kept him waiting in the hotel lounge while she changed into her evening dress.

Agatha Christie never spoke about the missing eleven days of her life and over the years there has been much speculation about what really happened between 3 and 14 December 1926.

Her husband said that she'd suffered a total memory loss as a result of the car crash. But according to biographer Andrew

Norman, the novelist may well have been in what's known as a 'fugue' state or, more technically, a psychogenic trance. It's a rare condition brought on by trauma or depression.

Norman says that her adoption of a new personality, Theresa Neele, and her failure to recognize herself in newspaper photographs were signs that she had fallen into psychogenic amnesia.

'I believe she was suicidal,' says Norman. 'Her state of mind was very low and she writes about it later through the character of Celia in her autobiographical novel *Unfinished Portrait*.'

She soon made a full recovery and once again picked up her writer's pen. But she was no longer prepared to tolerate her husband's philandering: she divorced him in 1928 and later married the distinguished archaeologist Sir Max Mallowan.

We'll probably never know for certain what happened in those lost eleven days. Agatha Christie left a mystery that even Hercule Poirot would have been unable to solve.

11

Dressed to Kill

Dressed in khaki fatigues and splattered in mud, Private Denis Smith looked little different from the thousands of other war-weary comrades.

The boyish face and cropped hair provoked few comments from those at the battlefront. Indeed, no one in the 51st Division of the Royal Engineers (British Expeditionary Force) knew that Private Smith was hiding an extraordinary secret.

He was actually a woman, Dorothy Lawrence, who had come to the battlefield to see with her own eyes what was taking place. In doing so, Lawrence became the only female soldier to fight on the Western Front in the First World War.

Dorothy's story began in Paris at the outbreak of war in 1914. She was desperate to become a war correspondent, but was told that it was a man's world in which she could play no part. Determined to witness the bloody fighting in Northern France, she decided to disguise herself as a soldier and make her own way to the front.

'I'll see what an ordinary English girl, without credentials or money, can accomplish,' she wrote.

She befriended two English soldiers in Paris – she later referred to them as her 'khaki accomplices' – and asked them to smuggle her a uniform. They agreed to help and within a week Dorothy was kitted out with military boots, khaki trousers, braces, jacket, a shirt and puttees.

There still remained the problem of how to disguise her feminine form. She knew that she would be arrested and sent home with immediate effect if anyone discovered that she was a woman.

'Enveloping myself in swathes of bandages, like a mummy, I pulled these swathes taut around my body.' But her womanly curves remained visible, 'so I padded my back with layers of cotton wool . . . my outfit revealed a thick-set and plump figure, finished by a somewhat small head and a boyish face'.

The men also helped her obtain an all-important travel pass that would enable her to reach the town of Béthune, which was right on the front line.

Concerned that she still looked too feminine, Dorothy had one of her accomplices crop her hair and shave her face. 'Vainly I hoped that boyish bristles would sprout,' she wrote. A born tomboy, she was disappointed when this failed to happen.

To complete her disguise before setting off for the front line, Dorothy coated her face in diluted Condy's fluid. Bronzed, and looking decidedly shabby, she now headed for the battlefront.

It was not easy to reach the fighting. On several occasions she was stopped by officers who demanded to know what she was doing so far from her supposed regiment. Yet none of them ever imagined she was a woman.

Dorothy eventually secured the services of a tunnel expert

named Sapper Tom Dunn who was serving with a Lancashire unit of the Royal Engineers. She admitted her secret to him and asked for his help.

Sapper Tom was amused by her daring and touched by her courage. He and a few comrades agreed to help get her into active service. They found her a secret hiding place where she could rest up during the day. Only when it became dark did she venture out with the other sappers, digging tunnels underneath the German lines and filling them with high explosive. The charges would then be set, blowing the German trenches and control centres high into the sky.

Hygiene was impossible and Dorothy was soon crawling with fleas and lice. 'Every inch of my body tickled and irritated,' she wrote. 'Fleas jumped in all directions.'

Although she faced terrible discomfort, she was soon actively involved in tunnelling underneath enemy lines. Shells and mortars rained down on her yet she never once flinched. Her closest male comrade, Sapper Tom, was extraordinarily impressed by her bravery. He later described how she spent ten continuous days and nights '400 yards from the Boche front line, under rifle fire and trench mortars'.

The incessant fire, poor food and contaminated water rapidly took its toll. Dorothy fell ill and suffered a series of fainting fits. Fearing that her ruse would be discovered, she presented herself to her commanding sergeant and admitted her deception. He immediately arrested her on suspicion of being a spy.

Intense interrogation followed. Six generals and twenty officers were involved in cross-questioning Dorothy, but failed to prove anything other than the fact that she was a woman who wanted to join the dangerous world of men.

They forced her to sign an affidavit to the effect that she would never write about her story. And then she was despatched back to London.

Dorothy did eventually write about her adventures and Sapper Dunn even signed an affidavit to vouch for the fact that it was true. Yet few believed her story and she died in obscurity in 1964.

12

Mission into Danger

Irena Sendler aroused no suspicion as she left the Warsaw ghetto with a parcel under her arm. As her dog barked noisily, she gripped the parcel more tightly and gave a friendly wave to the Gestapo guards. What they did not know – and they would have killed her if they had – was that she was smuggling Jewish babies to safety.

Sendler was a Polish Catholic social worker living in occupied Poland. She was permitted by the Nazi authorities to enter the Jewish ghetto in order to check for signs of typhus, for the Nazis were terrified of the disease spreading across the city.

Gestapo officials had no idea that they were being duped and that Irena Sendler was actually involved in one of the greatest rescue missions of all time. In the guise of an employee of the Social Services Department, she managed to smuggle some 2,500 Jewish children to safety.

Her work was extremely dangerous. Warsaw, in 1942, was full of Gestapo officers constantly searching for Jews who had managed to escape from the ghetto.

'Transporting weapons . . . planning sabotage against the Germans, none of it was as dangerous as hiding a Jew,' said Wladyslaw Bartoszewski of the Polish Resistance. 'You have a ticking time bomb in your home. If they find out, they will kill you, your family and the person you are hiding.'

Under the pretext of inspecting conditions in the ghetto, Sendler smuggled out babies and small children in packages, suitcases, boxes and trolleys. Older children were taken out through the city's sewers.

Irena always went into the ghetto with a dog, which she had trained to bark whenever German soldiers were about. This enabled her to cover any noises that the babies might make while they were wrapped up in her parcels. Once the children were safely out of the ghetto, they were given Catholic birth certificates and forged identity papers. These were signed by priests or officials who worked for the Social Services Department.

The children were then taken to orphanages and convents in the countryside around Warsaw.

By mid-1942, the SS were rounding up large numbers of Jews and transporting them to Treblinka extermination camp. Sendler begged Jewish parents to release their children, knowing it was their only hope of survival. In an interview recorded before her death in 2008, she spoke vividly of her conversations with the parents of these children.

'Those scenes over whether to give a child away were heart-rending . . . Their first question was: "What guarantee is there that the child will live?" I said, "None. I don't even know if I will get out of the ghetto alive today."'

Sendler kept a list of all those she had rescued and she secretly buried their names in jars. It was hoped that they would be reunited with their parents when the war was over.

In 1943, Sendler was arrested by the Gestapo. They'd grown suspicious of her activities and realized she was working on behalf of Warsaw's Jews. She was beaten, severely tortured by her guards (they broke her legs and arms) and then sentenced to death for refusing to give them any information.

News of her impending execution reached Żegota, the secret Council to Aid Jews, which managed to save her by bribing a German guard as she was being led away to be killed. She was listed on the bulletin boards as among those who'd been executed; this enabled her to live in hiding for the rest of the war.

At the war's end, Irena dug up jars containing the 2,500 children's identities in the hope of reuniting the youngsters with their parents. But almost all of the adults had been executed in Treblinka.

Irena found herself persecuted by Poland's post-war Communist authorities because of her relations with the Polish government-in-exile. Not until 1965 did she receive recognition for her extraordinary bravery. She was honoured as a 'righteous gentile' by the Israeli Holocaust Memorial Centre, Yad Vashem.

With the fall of Communism came recognition in her own land: many of Poland's highest honours were bestowed on her. In 2007, she was even nominated for the Nobel Peace Prize. But she did not win: the prize went to former Vice President Al Gore for his work on climate change.

Irena remained modest to her dying day. When asked about her work, she said simply: 'Every child saved with my help is the justification of my existence on this Earth, and not a title to glory.'

PART V

Man's Best Friend

America entered the war . . . and Stubby came to the conclusion that he ought to do his bit by his country.

NEW YORK TIMES OBITUARY OF SERGEANT STUBBY, THE MOST DECORATED DOG IN AMERICAN HISTORY, APRIL 1926.

13

The Real War Horse

He stood fearless and proud in readiness for the battle ahead. He had already braved four years of warfare, including the Battle of the Somme in 1916. He had also survived the muddy hell of Passchendaele. Now, on 30 March 1918, Warrior was to face his toughest assignment. The ten-year-old chestnut-brown gelding was to lead one of the last great cavalry charges in history.

His mission was to stop the German Spring Offensive of 1918 and his adventures were to prove every bit as extraordinary as those of Michael Morpurgo's fictional warhorse.

Warrior was one of the million horses sent to France between 1914 and 1918. Only 62,000 of them ever returned home. They are forgotten victims of a conflict that pitted defenceless animals against tanks and machine guns.

Warrior belonged to General John Seely, one of Churchill's closest friends, and both he and his horse were born survivors. Warrior had proved his mettle on numerous occasions since arriving in France in the summer of 1914. That autumn, he narrowly escaped capture by the advancing German army. In the following year, the horse next to him was killed when a shell exploded and ripped it in two. Warrior was extremely fortunate to escape unscathed.

A few days later, his stable was destroyed within seconds of him leaving it. On another occasion, he had to be dug out of mud that was several feet deep.

In February 1915, General Seely (and Warrior) were put in command of the Canadian Cavalry, a ragbag force of ranchers, Mounties, Native Americans and a thousand horses. After three years proving their worth on the battlefield, they were given a mission of vital strategic importance. The German war machine had broken through the Allied front line and taken more than 100,000 prisoners, many of them members of the British Fifth Army. Buoyed by this victory, the Germans were intent on pushing even further west.

It was vital that their advance should be checked as soon as possible. Allied forces were to take the offensive at Moreuil Wood on the banks of the Avre River. Victory here would not only secure the river but it would also stop the German thrust westwards.

The woodland attack was to take place on 30 March and to be led by Warrior and eleven other horses. Their initial task was to plant a red pennant on the hill above the river. This would act as a guide for the rest of the cavalry.

'[Warrior] was determined to go forward,' wrote Seely, 'and with a great leap started off. All sensation of fear vanished from him as he galloped at racing speed. There was a hail of bullets from the enemy as we crossed the intervening space and mounted the hill, but Warrior cared for nothing.'

Warrior made it to the hilltop and the pennant was planted.

Seconds later, there was a loud thundering as a thousand other horses followed him into battle.

Squadron after squadron rode into the chaos. Shells rained down on them and gunfire came spurting from every angle.

Warrior and his fellow horses advanced under protective covering fire from men of the Royal Flying Corps. More than 17,000 rounds were fired at the Germans. But it was to little avail: hundreds of horses were mown down by the German machine guns.

The battle continued into the late afternoon. Rain sluiced down from the metal-grey sky and the light soon began to fade. Warrior continued to lead the mounted brigade forward under continual fire until the battle slowly began to turn.

By nightfall, the wood had been captured and the Germans forced back. But victory came at a heavy price. A quarter of the men and more than half the horses had been killed in the bloodbath.

There was no respite for Warrior. He was called back into action on the following day in order to lead an attack close to the village of Gentelles. But he soon suffered such injuries that he had to be withdrawn. General Seely was also wounded and unable to continue the fight.

Warrior made a remarkable recovery and lived until 1941, too old to re-enter service in the Second World War. Besides, warfare had changed beyond all recognition in the intervening years. Cavalry charges belonged to the past and there was no longer a place for warhorses like Warrior.

He remains one of the unsung heroes of the Great War: a faithful, devoted and extraordinarily courageous warhorse who helped to secure victory on the Western Front.

14

Pigeon to the Rescue

Major Charles Whittlesey knew that the situation was desperate. Just twenty-four hours earlier, on 2 October 1918, he and his men had been ordered to advance against heavily fortified German positions in the Argonne Forest in Northern France. It was part of the biggest operation undertaken by the American Expeditionary Force in the First World War.

Charles Whittlesey was serving in the 77th Division, a motley band who were known as the Metropolitans, a reference to the fact that they had been drawn from New York's multi-ethnic Lower East Side. Between them they spoke forty-two languages.

The linguistic diversity did not hide the fact that most of the men were inexperienced soldiers. After brief but intensive training at Camp Upton in New York, they had been shipped to France. Some had not even learned how to throw a hand grenade.

Major Whittlesey was in command of 554 soldiers attacking the German front line. The strength of the enemy made this a perilous task, but what made it even more deadly was the hostile terrain.

The Argonne is an area of deep ravines and high bluffs of rock. It is easy to defend and almost impossible to attack. Whittlesley sniffed at the danger and sensed a tough time ahead. But orders were orders. On 2 October, he and his men moved forward.

They proved remarkably successful in penetrating the Argonne's ravines. Indeed, their initial success was to prove their downfall. The Allied units on their flanks were unable to make such rapid progress and it was not long before Major Whittlesey's men found themselves cut off. They had made the classic mistake of advancing too far.

The German counter-attack was devastating. Soldiers hidden on the high bluffs began firing downwards on Whittlesey's exposed positions, picking off the men below. They had no chance of firing back because the rocky pinnacles were two hundred feet high.

Whittlesey knew that any attempt to retreat would be tantamount to suicide. His men would be cut down by German machine guns. His only option was to sit tight until American forces could come to their aid.

His wireless equipment was unable to function in the gorge and his only means of contacting battlefield headquarters was to use one of the three carrier pigeons he had brought with him. When he learned that three hundred of his men had been killed, he sent one of the pigeons to headquarters with the message: 'Many wounded. We cannot evacuate.'

The pigeon was immediately shot down by the Germans. They were determined to prevent additional troops coming to Whittlesey's rescue.

The major sent his second pigeon: 'Men are suffering. Can

support be sent?' It was all to no avail: the second bird was also shot down.

Whittlesey had just one pigeon left, his prize bird, Cher Ami. He now desperately needed to send a message, for as well as being attacked by the Germans, his men were also coming under friendly fire from American artillery.

Whittlesey placed a note inside a canister and then attached it to Cher Ami's leg. 'We are along the road parallel to 276.4. Our own artillery is dropping a barrage directly on us. For heaven's sake, stop it!'

The men watched anxiously as Cher Ami began flying out of the ravine. He represented their last hope of salvation.

He was scarcely above the line of trees when he was spotted by German gunners. There was a burst of gunfire as they turned all their weaponry on him, firing wildly in an attempt to bring him down.

Cher Ami continued flying through the hail of bullets until disaster struck. The bird was hit and could be seen dropping to the ground. Major Whittlesey's men were devastated. They now knew that they were destined to die in this Argonne hellhole.

But no sooner had the gunfire stopped when there was a collective gasp. Cher Ami had struggled back into the air and was once again flying through the ravine. This time, he made it out alive.

Sixty-five minutes later, divisional headquarters sighted a carrier pigeon approaching its loft. It was Cher Ami. When they went to look for the message, they discovered he'd been shot through the breast and was blinded in one eye. One of his legs, the one carrying Major Whittlesey's message, was hanging from a single tendon. Divisional headquarters acted immediately and ordered an immediate halt to the bombardment.

The troops in the ravine managed to hold out for a further four days before the Allies finally sent in a relief force. The Germans retreated and Whittlesey's Lost Battalion, as it was already being called, was finally safe. Whittlesey returned to America a war hero. His stand in the Argonne became the stuff of legend.

Cher Ami was also to become a national hero. One of six hundred pigeons used by the United States Army Signal Corps, he had already delivered twelve important messages at Verdun. Now, his rescue of the Lost Battalion was his finest hour.

His leg was so damaged that it had to be amputated; a wooden leg was specially carved for him. And then he sailed back to America, with General John J. Pershing seeing him off personally.

On arrival, he was awarded the Croix de Guerre medal with a palm Oak Leaf Cluster; he would later become an exalted member of the Racing Pigeon Hall of Fame.

Cher Ami died on 13 June 1919, from wounds received in battle. He was stuffed by a taxidermist and placed on display in the Smithsonian, alongside another famous hero from the First World War, the mongrel dog Sergeant Stubby. Both of them remain there to this day.

15

Barking for Victory

It was a most unusual way to join the US Army. But then again, he was a most unusual recruit. Stubby sauntered onto the Connecticut training ground of the 102nd Infantry Division, wagged his tail and signalled his desire to serve in the First World War. It was the beginning of a long and illustrious canine military career.

Stubby was a brindle puppy with a short tail. Homeless and apparently ownerless, he was adopted by Private J. Robert Conroy and began training with the 102nd Infantry's 26 Yankee Division.

He proved quick to learn. Within weeks he knew all the bugle calls and drills and had even learned to salute his superiors, placing his right paw on his right eyebrow.

The time soon came for the Infantry Division to sail for France. Stubby ought to have been left behind, but Private Conroy smuggled him aboard the *SS Minnesota*. He was kept hidden in a coal bin until the ship was far out at sea; he was then brought out and introduced to the sailors, who were amused by his canine salutes.

When the ship arrived in France, Private Conroy smuggled him ashore. His commanding officer was minded to have the dog sent back on board, but he changed his mind when Stubby gave him a full military salute.

The Yankee Division headed for the front lines at Chemin des Dames, near Soissons, in the first week of February 1918. Stubby was allowed to accompany them as the division's official mascot. Under constant fire for over a month, he soon became used to the noise of shelling.

His first injury came not from gunfire but from poison gas. He was rushed to a field hospital and given emergency treatment. The gassing left him sensitive to even minute traces of the substance in the atmosphere. When the Infantry Division was the target of an early morning gas attack, the men were asleep and their lives were at great risk. But Stubby recognized the smell and ran through the trench barking and biting the soldiers in order to wake them. In doing so, he saved them from certain death.

Stubby also proved extraordinarily talented at finding wounded soldiers lying out in no man's land between the trenches of the opposing armies. He would stand by the body, barking loudly until stretcher bearers were able to rescue the injured person.

On one occasion, while serving in the Argonne, Stubby stumbled across a German soldier-spy who was in the process of mapping the layout of the Allied trenches. He understood what the man was doing and began barking wildly.

The German spy realized that his cover was blown and started to run back to his own trenches. But Stubby chased after the man, gnawing his legs and causing him to fall to the ground. He then pressed home his attack until American troops arrived and captured the spy.

Stubby's heroism in the face of extreme danger caused a

sensation. He was immediately promoted to the rank of sergeant by the commander of the 102nd Infantry.

A few months later, Sergeant Stubby was badly injured during a grenade attack and received a large amount of shrapnel in his chest and leg. He was rushed to a field hospital for emergency surgery then taken to a Red Cross hospital for additional treatment. When he was well enough to wander through the wards, he visited wounded soldiers, boosting their morale.

By the end of the war, Stubby had served in seventeen battles and four major offensives. He also played an important role in liberating Château-Thierry. The women of the town were so grateful that they made him a special chamois coat on which he could pin his many medals.

His military decorations included three service stripes, the French Battle of Verdun Medal, New Haven World War I Veterans Medal, Republic of France Grande Guerre Medal and the Château-Thierry campaign medal. He was also made a life member of the American Legion, the Red Cross and the YMCA. When the Humane Education Society awarded him a gold medal in 1921, it was presented by General John Pershing.

After the war, Stubby became a national celebrity, attending military parades up and down the country. He even got to meet three presidents: Wilson, Harding and Coolidge.

In 1926, he died peacefully in Private Conroy's arms. Brave, but also lucky, he was the most decorated dog of the First World War. He was also the only dog to be promoted to the rank of sergeant through combat.

PART VI

Guilty Until Proven Innocent

'I have nothing to say.'

AMELIA DYER, AS THE NOOSE WAS PLACED
AROUND HER NECK IN PREPARATION FOR
HER EXECUTION, 10 JUNE 1896

16

Angel of Death

It began with an advert in the Bristol *Times and Mirror*. 'Wanted,' it read, 'respectable woman to take young child.' The advertisement had been placed in the newspaper by Evelina Marmon, a twenty-five-year-old barmaid.

Two months earlier, in January 1896, Evelina had given birth to a baby girl named Doris. Unable to meet the cost of feeding and clothing the child, and abandoned by the man who made her pregnant, Evelina had no option but to find a foster home.

As she read through the advert she'd placed in the newspaper, her eye happened to fall on another advertisement on the same page. 'Married couple with no family would adopt healthy child, nice country home. Terms, £10.'

Foster families were not unusual in Victorian Britain. Unwanted pregnancies and poverty had led to a veritable foster industry, with thousands of illegitimate children being discreetly farmed out to charitable families. The mother of the unwanted child would pay a fee – it was either a one-off payment or a monthly advance – and find herself free of the stigma of having a child born out of wedlock.

Evelina, a vivacious blonde, read the advert and had the feeling that she was at last in luck. She immediately wrote to the lady – a Mrs Harding from Oxford Road in Reading – and asked for more information.

A reply was immediately forthcoming. 'I should be glad to have a dear little baby girl, one I could bring up and call my own,' wrote Mrs Harding. She also provided a little more information about her love of children. 'We are plain, homely people, in fairly good circumstances. I don't want a child for money's sake, but for company and home comfort. Myself and my husband are dearly fond of children. I have no child of my own. A child with me will have a good home and a mother's love.'

Evelina was thrilled by what she read; it was the answer to all her prayers. Mrs Harding even described the enchanting place where she and her husband lived. There was a large garden and an orchard. It was the perfect place to raise a young child.

There was only one detail that caused Evelina a moment's hesitation. Mrs Harding said she could not accept a weekly fee for caring for baby Doris. Rather, she wanted a one-off payment of £10. She said she would take entire responsibility for the child and that Evelina would never have to trouble herself about the illegitimate baby.

Evelina felt uneasy. As with any young mother, the idea of being separated forever from her newborn was extremely painful. But she was in such desperate straits that she agreed to Mrs Harding's terms. A week later, Mrs Harding arrived in Cheltenham to pick up baby Doris.

And this was the point when Evelina got a most unwelcome surprise. She was expecting Mrs Harding to be youthful and maternal. Instead, she turned out to be an elderly woman with a rough-looking face.

Evelina was somewhat reassured by the loving way Mrs Harding picked up the baby. She wrapped Doris tightly in a shawl, professing to be concerned about the chill evening air. After chatting about the wonderful home in which the baby would be brought up, she turned to leave. Evelina shed a quiet tear as she waved farewell.

A few days later Evelina wrote to Mrs Harding for news of baby Doris and was relieved to learn that all was well. But it was to be the last news she ever heard of her baby. All of her subsequent letters went unanswered – and with good reason. Baby Doris was dead.

Only much later would the grisly story emerge, one that would cause shock and revulsion throughout Victorian Britain. Mrs Harding was not who she claimed to be; her real name was Amelia Dyer. Under the pretence of being a foster mother, she took in illegitimate babies (for a sizeable fee) and then murdered them.

Amelia Dyer did not take baby Doris home to Reading as she had promised. Instead, she went directly to Mayo Road in Willesden where her daughter lived. In the room upstairs, she took some white edging tape from a box and wound it tightly around baby Doris's neck, slowly strangling the child. She pawned Doris's baby clothes, thereby earning herself a few more shillings, and then wrapped the corpse in a napkin.

On the following morning, she took delivery of another child, a thirteen-month-old boy named Harry Simmons. He, too, was strangled.

The next evening, Dyer shoved the two corpses into an old carpet bag and threw it into a lonely spot by the weir at Caversham Lock. Unknown to her, it did not sink.

Nor did she know that she was already under police surveillance. Just days before killing baby Doris, the police had recovered a parcel in the Thames, near Reading. On opening it, they found the remains of a baby. Crucially, they also found the smudged remnants of an old label on the parcel. After a clever piece of detective work, police found themselves on the trail of Amelia Dyer.

Suspecting Dyer of murdering babies, the police began dragging a stretch of river. They pulled out three baby corpses, followed by the bag that contained the remains of Doris Marmon and Harry Simmons.

In the third week of May, Amelia Dyer was put on trial for murder. She pleaded guilty to one of the killings, baby Doris, and claimed insanity as her defence.

This was swiftly rejected. The jury took just four-and-a-half minutes to find her guilty and Amelia was hanged two weeks later. To the surprise of many, her daughter escaped prosecution.

The police never discovered how many other babies Amelia had killed, but the vast collection of baby clothes and letters found at her house suggested that she had murdered many more. Indeed, some believed her to have killed more than four hundred babies, making her the most prolific murderess in history.

17

Who Killed Rasputin?

The frozen corpse was spotted in the River Neva on the last day of December 1916. A river policeman noticed a fur coat lodged beneath the ice and ordered the surface crust to be broken.

The frozen body was immediately recognizable as belonging to Grigori Rasputin, 'holy' adviser to the tsar and tsarina of Russia. Tsar Nicholas and his wife, Alexandra, believed Rasputin to be blessed with semi-magical powers that brought temporary relief to their haemophiliac son.

Others took a rather different view. Rasputin was widely hated as a dissolute fraudster who was manipulating the affairs of state to his own advantage. Many in the Russian capital had long wished him dead.

The corpse was prised from its icy sepulchre and taken to Chesmenskii Hospice. Here, a post-mortem was undertaken by Professor Dmitrii Kosorotov. Rumours about Rasputin's death were already circulating around Petrograd, rumours that would later be fuelled by one of the murderers. Prince Felix Yusupov, in whose palace Rasputin had died, not only admitted to being involved, but also justified the killing by arguing that Rasputin was bad for Russia. He bragged about having poisoned him with cyanide before shooting him through the heart.

'He rushed at me, trying to get at my throat, and sank his fingers into my shoulder like steel claws. His eyes were bursting from their sockets, blood oozed from his lips.'

From the outset there were good reasons to doubt Yusupov's account. The professor conducting the post-mortem noted that the corpse was in a terrible state of mutilation. 'His left side has a weeping wound, due to some sort of slicing object or a sword. His right eye has come out of its cavity and falls down onto his face . . . His right ear is hanging down and torn. His neck has a wound from some sort of rope tie. The victim's face and body carry traces of blows given by a supple but hard object.'

Rasputin had been repeatedly beaten with a heavy cosh.

More horrifying was the damage to his genitals. At some point, his legs had been wrenched apart and his testicles had been 'crushed by the action of a similar object'.

Other details gleaned by Professor Kosorotov suggest that Yusupov's account was nothing more than fantasy. The story of the poisoned cakes was untrue; the post-mortem found no trace of poison in Rasputin's stomach.

Kosorotov also examined the three bullet wounds in Rasputin's body. 'The first has penetrated the left side of the chest and has gone through the stomach and liver. The second has entered into the right side of the back and gone through the kidney.'

Both of these would have inflicted terrible wounds, but the third bullet was the fatal shot. '[It] hit the victim in the forehead and penetrated into his brain.' Professor Kosorotov noted, significantly, that the bullets 'came from different calibre revolvers'.

On the night of the murder, Yusupov was in possession of a pocket Browning, as was fellow conspirator Grand Duke Dmitrii. Vladimir Purishkevich, also present, had a Savage.

These weapons could have caused the wounds to Rasputin's liver and kidney. But the fatal gunshot wound to Rasputin's head could only have come from a revolver. Ballistic experts now agree that the grazing around the wound is consistent with that left by a lead, non-jacketed bullet fired at point-blank range.

All the evidence points to the fact that the gun was a British-made .455 Webley revolver. This was the gun that belonged to Oswald Rayner, a close friend of Yusupov since the days when they had both studied at Oxford University.

Unknown to anyone except the small group of conspirators, Rayner had also been present on the night of Rasputin's murder. Sent to Russia more than a year earlier, he was a British agent working for the Secret Intelligence Service (now MI6).

Prince Yusupov was circumspect about Rayner when he wrote his memoirs. He mentions meeting him on the day after Rasputin's murder but presents their meeting as a chance encounter. 'I met my friend Oswald Rayner . . . he knew of our conspiracy and had come in search of news.'

Yusupov did indeed meet with Rayner after the murder, but Rayner had not needed to 'come in search of news' for he had fired the fatal shot.

Rayner would later tell his family that he was present in the Yusupov palace that night, information that would eventually find its way into his obituary. Surviving letters from his fellow agents also shed light on his role. 'A few awkward questions have already been asked about wider involvement,' wrote one. 'Rayner is attending to loose ends.'

The tsar was quick to hear rumours of British involvement in

Rasputin's murder. Anxious to know more, he asked the British ambassador if Rayner had a hand in the killing.

The ambassador denied any knowledge of Rayner's involvement. So, too, did Samuel Hoare, the head of the British espionage bureau in Petrograd. 'An outrageous charge', he said, 'and incredible to the point of childishness.'

Yet Hoare was remarkably quick to learn of Rasputin's death. Indeed he telegrammed London with news of the murder many hours before it was publicly known in Petrograd.

18

Till Death Us Do Part

The letter begins as an intimate billet-doux. 'Oh Harry, my own precious darling, your letter today is one long yearning cry for your little love.'

But within a few lines, a more sinister story begins to emerge. 'Yesterday, I administered the powder you left me . . . the result? Nil.'

The powder – arsenic – had not worked.

The writer of the letter was an Edwardian housewife named Augusta Fullam, who lived in Agra in central north India. Her 'precious darling' was Lieutenant Henry Clark, a surgeon. Together, in 1911, the two lovers decided to poison Augusta's husband Edward. Once he was dead, they would then kill Mrs Clark, Henry's wife. And then they would get married.

But they found themselves with a significant problem when they tried to kill Edward – he stubbornly refused to die. Each day, Augusta sprinkled arsenic powder onto his supper or slipped it into his tea, but all to no avail. 'My hubby returned the whole jug of tea saying it tasted bad,' she wrote in one letter to her lover.

On Friday 16 June 1911, Augusta managed to administer a massive dose to her husband. This time he ate the lot. But once again, it failed to kill him. 'Since 4pm [he's] vomited eight times . . . vomited ten times at a quarter to nine . . . vomited 12 times at ten pm.'

Augusta began to fear that he was indestructible. 'I give him half a tonic powder every day in his Sanatogen, lovie darling, because it lays on the top of the white powder quite unsuspiciously.'

For month after month, Augusta fed her husband arsenic. And for month after month Edward clung to life, despite vomiting many times each day. But eventually he fell seriously ill. As he lay in bed with a raging fever, Lieutenant Clark decided to finish him off with a huge dose of poison, administering it himself. Within hours, Edward Fullam was dead.

In his capacity as surgeon, Lieutenant Clark was able to sign the death certificate; it recorded the cause of death as heart failure.

The lovers were halfway to their goal. All they now had to do was murder Mrs Clark. This time, they decided not to waste months in administrating arsenic. Instead, Lieutenant Clark hired four assassins who broke into the house and struck Louisa Clark with a sword, smashing her skull. The noise of the brutal attack woke the Clarks' daughter, Maud, who screamed, causing the robbers to flee.

Agra police began their investigations that same day and their suspicions immediately fell on Lieutenant Clark and Augusta Fullam. Their love affair had not gone unnoticed in the local community and they clearly had a motive for both murders. But the detectives assigned to the case could find no conclusive proof.

None, that is, until Inspector Smith called at Augusta Fullam's house and noticed a large metal box hidden under the bed.

When he asked what was inside, Augusta turned bright red 'and fell like a heap into a chair'.

Inspector Smith had the box prised open; inside there were 370 love letters that set down in great detail how Augusta and Lieutenant Clark had planned their terrible crime.

The ensuing trial proved a sensation – colonial India had never before seen such a spectacular double murder. Every sordid detail was splashed across both the Indian and British newspapers.

The two lovers were tried separately and both were convicted. Lieutenant Clark was hanged on Wednesday 26 March 1913. Augusta Fullam, who was pregnant at the time of the trial, was sentenced to life. She served just fifteen months before dying of heatstroke the following year.

'My very own precious lovie,' she had written when she and Clark first started administering the arsenic, 'don't you think our correspondence rather risky?'

But Lieutenant Clark assured her it was fine. He said they would never be caught.

PART VII

Big-Time Adventure

I was listening to the radio when [the newscasters] told about it. I cut my iron off and I run to my neighbors house and said: 'Did you hear what was on the radio? My brothers have escaped from Alcatraz.'

MARIE WIDNER, SISTER OF ESCAPING PRISONERS,
JOHN AND CLARENCE ANGLIN

19

By Balloon to the North Pole

At exactly 2.30 p.m. on 11 July 1897, a gigantic silk balloon could be seen rising into the Arctic sky above Spitsbergen. Inside the basket were three hardy adventurers, all Swedish, who were taking part in an extraordinary voyage.

Salomon Andrée was the instigator of the mission. Charismatic and confident, he managed to persuade Nils Strindberg and Knut Fraenkel to accompany him on his historic balloon flight over the North Pole.

Andrée was confident of success. His balloon, the *Eagle*, used advanced hydrogen technology and he claimed to have developed a revolutionary steering system using drag-ropes.

A disastrous test flight suggested that Andrée's confidence was seriously misplaced. The much-vaunted rope-steerage system had numerous glitches and hydrogen was found to be seeping out of the balloon's 8-million little stitching-holes.

The expedition ought to have been abandoned before it even took off. But Andrée overruled all objections and the launch was scheduled for the second week of July.

The problems began within minutes of getting airborne. As the balloon drifted across the sea to the north of Spitsbergen, it was weighed down by the weight of the drag-ropes – so much so that at one point the balloon actually dipped into the water.

Andrée jettisoned 530 kilograms of ropes, along with 210 kilograms of ballast. This lightened the balloon so much that it now rose too high. The change in air pressure caused huge quantities of hydrogen to escape through the stitching-holes. Andrée remained optimistic, releasing a carrier pigeon with the message: 'All well on board'.

This was far from true. The first ten hours of troubled flight were followed by forty-one hours in which the balloon, soaked in a rainstorm, flew so low that it kept bumping into the frozen sea.

The *Eagle* eventually crash-landed onto sea-ice some fifty hours after taking off from Spitsbergen. No one was hurt, but it was clear that the balloon would never fly again. The men were stranded, many miles from anywhere and lost in an Arctic wilderness.

They were well equipped with safety equipment including guns, sleds, skis, a tent and a small boat. Yet returning to the relative safety of Spitsbergen involved a gruelling march across shifting, melting ice.

The men spent a week at the crash site before setting out on their long hike. They had a reasonable quantity of food including meat, sausages and pemmican, but found it impossible to transport so much weight across the rucked-up ice. Much of the food had to be abandoned. Henceforth, they were to rely on hunting for their survival.

They left their makeshift camp on 22 July and initially headed for Franz Josef Land. But the ice soon became impassable so they headed instead towards the Seven Islands, a seven-week march, where there was known to be a depot of food.

The terrain was so gruelling that they were reduced to advancing on all fours. But they eventually reached a place where the sea-ice had melted sufficiently for them to use their collapsible boat.

'Paradise!' wrote Andrée in his diary. 'Large even ice floes with pools of sweet drinking water and here and there a tender-fleshed young polar bear!'

Their passage soon became impassable once again, forcing them to change direction. Aware that winter would soon be upon them, they built a hut upon an ice floe. But the ice broke up beneath them and they were lucky to struggle ashore onto desolate Kvitøya Island.

'Morale remains good,' reported Andrée. 'With such comrades as these, one ought to be able to manage under practically any circumstances whatsoever.' It was the last coherent message he ever wrote. Within a few days, all three men were dead.

Their fate was to become one of the great mysteries of Arctic exploration. What happened to them? They had shelter, food and ammunition and ought to have been able to keep themselves alive. In the absence of any news, the world's media began to speculate on their fate.

It was not until 1930, fully thirty-three years after the men were lost, that their remains were finally found. Far from answering questions, the discovery of their bodies only deepened the mystery.

The most plausible theory is that the men died of trichinosis, contracted after eating undercooked polar bear meat. They certainly had the symptoms of the disease and larvae of the *Trichinella* parasite were found in a polar bear carcass at the site. But recent scientific evidence has thrown doubt on this theory.

Other suggestions include vitamin A poisoning from eating

polar bear liver, lead poisoning from the food cans or carbon dioxide poisoning from their Primus stove.

By the time they struggled ashore they were living off scant quantities of canned goods from the balloon stores, along with portions of half-cooked polar bear meat.

They were suffering from foot pains and debilitating diarrhoea and were constantly cold and exhausted. Indeed they were so weary on their arrival at Kvitøya Island that they left much of their valuable equipment down by the water's edge.

Nils Strindberg, the youngest, was the first to die. His corpse was wedged into a crack in the cliff. Analysis of his clothing suggests he was killed by a polar bear.

The other two men seem to have weakened dramatically in the days that followed Strindberg's death. As the Arctic winter struck in earnest, they lost the will to live.

It will never be known how many days they survived in their makeshift Arctic shack. By the time they were eventually found, all that remained was their diaries, a few spools of undeveloped film and a heap of bleached bones.

20

Escape from Alcatraz

It was a routine inspection by the prison warders. On the morning of 12 June 1962, the guards at Alcatraz high security prison made their morning check on the prisoners in their cells.

When they came to Cell Block B, they quickly realized that something was not quite right. The men were in their beds, but they were showing no signs of life.

The guards unlocked the cells and were stunned by what they found. Frank Morris, John Anglin and Clarence Anglin were missing; in their place were elaborately made papier-mâché heads with real hair and painted eyes. Three of Alcatraz's most dangerous prisoners had escaped.

Neither the guards nor the other prisoners could believe that they'd managed to get away. Alcatraz, after all, was one of the world's most closely guarded prisons. Situated on a rocky island in San Francisco Bay, it was washed by cold and hazardous waters, making escape almost impossible.

In its twenty-nine years as a federal prison, from 1934 to 1963, no one had ever made it out alive. Forty-one inmates tried. Of those, twenty-six were recaptured, seven were shot dead and at least three were known to have drowned.

This proved no deterrent for the three new escapees. In fact, they saw the island's isolation as a challenge.

All three men were hardened criminals. Frank Morris had first been convicted at the age of thirteen. Since that time, he'd been involved in a number of serious crimes ranging from armed robbery to dealing in narcotics. He had been transferred to Alcatraz in 1960.

John Anglin was also an infamous criminal. He'd robbed the Columbia Alabama Bank in 1958, together with his two brothers. It had earned him a thirty-five-year prison sentence.

Clarence Anglin had been involved in a number of other bank robberies and had also been caught escaping from the Atlanta State Penitentiary. It was decided to send him to Alcatraz, in order to prevent him from making any more escape attempts.

All of the men were highly resourceful and extremely motivated. They discovered that there was an unguarded three-foot-wide utility corridor behind their cells. This led to an air vent and thence to the outside world. The prisoners began to chisel away at the moisture-damaged concrete. For tools, they used metal spoons stolen from the canteen and an electric drill that they improvised from the motor of a stolen vacuum cleaner. They did most of the work during music hour, when the noise of accordions covered the sound of their hacking at the concrete.

They also made dummy heads from soap, toilet paper and real hair in order to fool the guards; there were constant checks on the prisoners throughout the night.

It took a year to tunnel through the wall of the service tunnel. The men then had to steal a long piece of cord in order to reach the manhole that covered the air vent. When they finally lifted the manhole cover, they replaced the metal bolts with fake ones made of soap. Finally, on the night of 11 June, all was ready. It was time to make their escape.

Everything went exactly to plan. They crawled into the utility corridor, climbed the air vent and reached the prison roof. Then they clambered down to the rocky ground and began pumping air into a raft that they'd previously made from rubber raincoats. They'd even managed to make oars.

What happened next is a complete mystery. The three men disappeared and were never seen again. They were never captured, despite an extraordinary FBI manhunt, and nor were their bodies ever found.

Their raft was washed up on the following day on Angel Island, some two miles from Alcatraz, and there were footprints leading away from the raft. But there the trail went cold. Did they drown? Did they get away? These are questions that no one has ever been able to answer.

A recent investigation discovered that a car was stolen on the very night of the escape; the prisoners had always intended to make their getaway by car. But despite an exhaustive investigation, detectives are no closer to solving the mystery.

If they survived, the escapees would now be in their eighties. This does not mean that the case has been closed. According to US Marshal Michael Dyke, 'There's an active warrant and the Marshals Service doesn't give up looking for people . . . There's no proof they're dead, so we're not going to quit looking.'

And so the search goes on. The FBI website requests anyone with any information regarding the prison's greatest escape to call (415) 436-7677.

21

A Lonely Trek Through the Andes

There was a sickening crunch and a violent jerk. The right wing of the plane was ripped off by the mountain peak and flung backwards into the rear of the fuselage. The plane, wildly out of control, smashed into a second peak, which tore off the left wing.

Inside the cabin, the terrified passengers expected the shattered plane to plunge them to their deaths. But the plane's crash-landing miraculously spared some of those on board. The fuselage hit a snow-covered mountain slope and slid downwards before coming to a halt in a deep drift.

As a wall of silence descended over the wreckage, the injured and groaning survivors came to their senses. They were lost in the wilds of the High Andes. But they were alive.

There had been forty-five people on board Uruguayan Air Force flight 571 when it took off on Friday 13 October 1972. Among the passengers was the Old Christians Club rugby team from Montevideo, en route to Chile.

As the injured survivors clambered from the wreckage they

found that thirty-eight of them were still alive, although several were suffering from such injuries that they would clearly not survive for long.

Their pitiful plight soon struck home. They were lost in the snowbound Andes at an altitude of more than 3,600 metres with no food or winter clothing. Worse still, they lacked any medical supplies – a major handicap given that many of them were suffering from wounds sustained in the crash.

They gathered together the remaining food on board. It did not amount to much: some snacks, a little chocolate and a few bottles of wine. There was nothing to eat on the windswept mountains, nor any animals to hunt.

'At high altitude, the body's caloric needs are astronomical . . .' wrote Nando Parrado, one of the survivors. 'We were starving in earnest, with no hope of finding food, but our hunger soon grew so voracious that we searched anyway . . . Again and again we scoured the fuselage in search of crumbs and morsels . . . Again and again I came to the same conclusion – unless we wanted to eat the clothes we were wearing, there was nothing here but aluminium, plastic, ice, and rock.'

It became clear that if they were to survive, they would have to eat their dead loved ones. It was a decision that was not taken lightly. Many of those aboard the plane were strict Roman Catholics who had serious reservations about resorting to cannibalism. But they also knew they had little choice. Unless they ate, they would die.

Among the crash survivors was Roberto Canessa, a young medical student. He was convinced that a small party should try to hike over the mountains and seek help. This would involve a gruelling trek over some of the world's most inhospitable terrain. They would have to climb peaks of almost 5,000 metres. They would also face extreme temperatures with no winter clothing. Worse still, they would have almost no food.

After waiting eight weeks for the temperatures to rise a little, Roberto Canessa and two comrades, Nando Parrado and Antonio Vizintin, set off on their long march. It was 12 December.

The lack of oxygen was their first hazard. The constant climbing left them dizzy and desperately short of breath. The cold, too, was hard to endure. They had made a makeshift sleeping bag, but the nights were nevertheless bitter.

Parrado was the fittest; he reached the peak of the first high mountain before the other two. From the top, he got the shock of his life. He thought they'd crashed just a few miles from the Chilean border and was expecting to see some distant signs of civilization. Instead, he saw nothing but a barren vista of ice-bound mountains and valleys stretching for as far as the eye could see.

Only now did the men realize that they'd crashed in the middle of the High Andes and were a vast distance from the nearest human habitation.

Aware that the rescue hike would be even more arduous than anticipated, Vizintin chose to head back to the crash site. The others continued on their long trek. For day after day they crossed lonely peaks and valleys. They were freezing at night and constantly starved. But they eventually found a stream that led them out of their frozen hell. After nine days of gruelling marching along the banks of the Rio Azufre, they saw cows – a sure sign of human habitation.

As they prepared to make a fire that evening, Canessa looked up and noticed a man on the far side of the river. He shouted and waved, trying to show that they desperately needed help. Over the roar of the water they heard him shout 'tomorrow'.

The two survivors slept soundly that night, aware that their ordeal was almost at an end. On the following day, the Chilean horseman brought them some bread and hurled it across the river, along with a pen and paper. They wrote down what had happened and flung it back.

The horseman went back to raise the alarm and get help for Canessa and Parrado. Shortly afterwards they were finally rescued and given much needed shelter, food and water.

That same day, 22 December, two helicopters set off for the crash site. Despite atrocious weather they eventually plucked the remaining survivors from the mountain. They were in a desperate state: cold, starving and suffering from extreme malnutrition.

But sixteen of them had survived seventy-two days without food and supplies in one of the bleakest spots on earth.

PART VIII

I'm a Celebrity

'One of Captain Loewenstein's secretaries came into my cabin and handed me a piece of paper on which I read: Mr Loewenstein has fallen out of the plane.'

PILOT DONALD DREW, INTERVIEWED BY *THE TIMES*,
JULY 1928.

22

The First Celebrity Kidnap

At around 10 p.m. on 1 March 1932, nursemaid Betty Gow went to make a final check on twenty-month-old Charles Lindbergh, son of the famous aviator of the same name.

To her surprise, she found that baby Charles was missing from his cot. She went straightaway to seek out his mother, Anne, to see if she had taken him.

Anne didn't have the baby, so Betty went to see Charles, who was in his study.

He didn't have the baby either and he was alarmed to hear that Charles junior was missing from his crib. He rushed up to the nursery to check for himself. Betty was right. The baby was missing.

As he looked around the room his eyes alighted on a white envelope that had been left close to the windowsill. Written in poor English it read:

Dear Sir! Have 50.000$ redy 25.000$ in 20$ bills 15.000$ in

10$ bills and 10.000$ in 5$ bills After 2–4 days we will inform you were to deliver the money.

The letter also warned him not to notify anyone of the abduction.

Lindbergh ignored the last warning and immediately called the police. They arrived twenty minutes later.

A thorough search of the kidnapping scene revealed smudged footprints underneath the nursery window. Two sections of ladder had been used to reach the window; these were found near the house.

One of the sections was split, suggesting that the ladder had broken during the descent. There were no bloodstains in or about the nursery, nor were there any fingerprints.

The Lindberghs were understandably distraught and desperate to get their baby back. Charles Lindbergh gave the police investigation every support, but he also made contact with a number of underworld characters in the hope they'd be able to trace his child. Two of these, Salvatore Spitale and Irving Bitz, immediately offered their services. But they also approached the *New York Daily News* in the hope of selling advance information on the baby-snatch.

On 6 March, five days after the kidnapping, Charles received a second ransom note. This increased the ransom demand to $70,000. It was followed by a third and fourth ransom note, at which point a trusted local ex-headmaster named Dr John F. Condon offered his services. He suggested trying to make direct contact with the kidnapper by placing a series of adverts in local newspapers. If the kidnapper responded to his adverts, he could act as an intermediary in any ransom negotiations.

It was a long shot but to everyone's surprise it worked. The kidnapper responded and, from this point on, all his notes were sent directly to Dr Condon.

One of these contained instructions for him to meet with an unidentified man called 'John' at Woodlawn Cemetery in New York. Dr Condon duly went along, met with 'John' and discussed payment of the ransom money. In return, the stranger handed Dr Condon the baby's sleeping suit, proof enough that he had little Charles. When the Lindberghs saw the sleeping suit, they immediately recognized it as belonging to their baby.

After an exchange of yet more notes, Dr Condon once again met with 'John'. He handed over $50,000 and was told that the kidnapped child could be found on a boat named *Nellie* near Martha's Vineyard, Massachusetts. An extensive search and rescue mission failed to find any boat of that name.

On 12 May, almost ten weeks after the kidnapping, the body of a baby was found, partly buried and decomposed, some five miles from the Lindberghs' home. Its head was crushed, there was a hole in the skull and the left leg and both hands were missing.

The body was positively identified as Charles Lindbergh and was cremated, at the Lindberghs' insistence, on the following day. The coroner concluded that the child had been dead for some two months and that the cause of death was a blow to the head.

The New Jersey State police were no nearer to finding the murderer, despite offering a ransom of $25,000. They knew that the most likely means of capturing the kidnapper was to ensnare him while trying to spend the ransom money, which had been paid in so-called gold certificates whose numbers had been noted by the police.

One suspicious gold certificate was spotted by a teller at a bank in the Bronx. It had a New York number plate, 4U-13-14-N.Y, pencilled in the margin. This helped police track the bill to a petrol station in Upper Manhattan. The station manager, Walter Lyle, recalled writing down the number because he thought the customer looked 'suspicious'.

The number plate led the police to a blue Dodge owned by a certain Bruno Hauptmann, aged thirty-five, a native of Saxony in Germany. He was arrested and when police searched his home they found almost $2,000 in those same gold certificates.

They also found a great deal of additional evidence. There was a notebook that contained a sketch for the construction of a collapsible ladder similar to that found at the Lindbergh home and they found that the wood in his loft was identical to the wood used to make the ladder. They also found Dr Condon's telephone number in his house.

The trial of Hauptmann began in January 1935. He was charged with extortion and murder. The evidence that had been found in his home, together with handwriting samples from the ransom notes, quickly secured his conviction. Although the defence appealed, the verdict was upheld and Hauptmann was electrocuted at 8.47 p.m. on 3 April 1936.

There have been many attempts to prove that he was duped, framed or otherwise innocent, but the most authoritative recent account, written by the former FBI agent Jim Fisher, concludes that 'Hauptmann is as guilty today as he was in 1932 when he kidnapped and killed the son of Mr. and Mrs. Charles Lindbergh.'

23

Sir Osman of Hyderabad

His personal fortune was said to be more than double the annual revenue of India and he owned enough pearls to pave Piccadilly from one end to the other. His jewels alone were worth a staggering £400 million.

Sir Osman Ali Khan, autocratic ruler of the princely state of Hyderabad, was once the richest man in the world and also a contender for one of the richest people in history.

He was worth more than £2 billion in 1940 and had an array of sumptuous palaces filled with rare and wonderful treasures: oriental carpets, priceless manuscripts and rare gemstones. He shared his wealth with his seven wives, forty-two concubines and vast numbers of children and dependants.

Every statistic about Sir Osman is eye-watering. He ruled a state that was just a fraction smaller than the UK and he held absolute power over the lives of 16 million people.

He had dozens of Rolls-Royces and owned the rare Jacob diamond, valued today at £100 million. He was also a fanatical ally of the British during the Raj and donated all the fighter planes that made up the Royal Flying Corp's 110 Squadron in the First World War.

The British responded by awarding him with the titles 'His Exalted Highness' and 'Faithful Ally of the British Government'.

Sir Osman had succeeded his father as ruler of Hyderabad on the latter's death in 1911. Already fabulously wealthy, he expanded the family coffers by increasing the mining industry in the state of Hyderabad. The mines were a rich source of diamonds and other precious stones. The famous Koh-i-Noor diamond came from Hyderabad.

By 1941, Sir Osman had founded his own bank, the Hyderabad State Bank. His fiefdom became the only state on the subcontinent that issued its own currency, quite different from that of the rest of India. Often benevolent, and always erratic, Sir Osman spent much of the family fortune on education, railways and electrification. But there was plenty of spare cash for him to indulge his passion for racehorses, rare cars and regal uniforms.

Huge sums of money were also spent on a lavish beautification programme that included public buildings, a high court, hospitals and the Osmania University. But Sir Osman's real passion remained his palaces, which were scattered across his realm. The biggest were staffed by many thousands of servants, retainers and bodyguards, all jostling for position alongside scheming eunuchs and jealous concubines.

Sir Osman's favourite palace was said to be the Falaknuma, built on a hilltop above Hyderabad with a panoramic view across the city. Known as 'Mirror of the Sky', it was constructed in the classical style out of imported Italian marble.

There was also the Chowmahalla Palace, another rambling edifice that had been started in 1750 and took another 120 years to complete. It became famous for its pillared Durbah Hall, a vast marble salon lit by chandeliers made of Belgian crystal. There were huge drawing rooms, courtyards and an elegant clock tower.

Sir Osman seemed to have had it all: a fortune, palaces and a peaceful dominion that managed to escape integration into the new Indian state. But everything was soon to turn sour. After months of failed negotiations with India, Sir Osman's fiefdom was invaded in 1948. There were five days of fighting before he reluctantly agreed to join the union. His autocratic rule was replaced by India's parliamentary democracy.

A quarter of a century later, Sir Osman's titles were abolished and he was subjected to crippling taxes.

His death in February 1967 was always going to result in a complex battle over inheritance. There were hundreds of would-be claimants to his land and property.

His grandson, Mukarram Jah, was his official successor, but he rapidly found himself in deep financial trouble. He inherited not only huge debts, but also an enormous number of servants, retainers and hangers-on. These included nearly 15,000 palace staff and dependants, along with the forty-two concubines and their numerous offspring.

The family's oldest and most prestigious palace, the Chowmahalla, still had 6,000 employees. Thirty-eight of them were employed solely to dust the chandeliers.

Thus began a complex and highly rancorous legal battle over Sir Osman's fortune, which had shrunk to a mere £1 billion at the time of his death. Mukarram Jah eventually tired of the wrangling and left India altogether. He divorced his first wife, the Turkish-born Princess Esra, and emigrated to Australia, where he became a sheep farmer.

And there the story ended, at least for more than twenty years. But in 2001, Princess Esra returned to India in a bid to sort out her grandfather-in-law's complex will. With the help of a gifted lawyer, the competing claims over the inheritance were finally resolved.

The beautiful Chowmahalla Palace was eventually re-opened as a museum and the Falaknuma became a luxury palace hotel. The many descendants of Sir Osman are now free to come back and reflect on the former glories of their once-noble family.

But these days, they have to pay like everyone else.

24

The Very Strange Death of Alfred Loewenstein

In the early evening of 4 July 1928, a fabulously wealthy businessman named Alfred Loewenstein boarded his private plane at Croydon Airport. It was a routine flight that would take him across the English and French coastlines before landing at Brussels, where Loewenstein lived with his wife, Madeleine.

Loewenstein was instantly recognizable to the staff at the airport. Indeed he was recognizable wherever he went. He was a spectacularly wealthy entrepreneur; so wealthy that he was widely known as the world's richest man.

Already rich before the First World War, his fortune had increased dramatically in the peace that followed. His various companies provided electric power for developing countries and before long he was being sought out by presidents and prime ministers around the globe.

But he also had many enemies. In 1926, he established International Holdings and Investments, which raised huge amounts of capital from wealthy investors. By 1928, these investors wanted some return on their money. And they wanted it sooner rather than later.

Loewenstein was pleased to be flying home on that July day in 1928. It was a fine evening for flying with scarcely a cloud in the sky. The pilot, Donald Drew, assured him that it would be a smooth flight.

There was a total of six people on the plane, in addition to Alfred Loewenstein. Pilot Drew stood by the doorway of the aircraft as the passengers and crew boarded. The other people in the cabin included Fred Baxter, Loewenstein's loyal valet, and Arthur Hodgson, his male secretary. There were also two women, Eileen Clarke and Paula Bidalon, his stenographers.

In the cockpit were Drew and Robert Little, the aircraft mechanic. The cockpit was a sealed unit with only a porthole connecting it to the rest of the plane. Once the Fokker had taken off, Drew and Little had no direct access to the cabin.

Shortly after 6 p.m., the Fokker FVII, a small monoplane, set off down the grass runway. Within minutes the plane was airborne and climbing to its cruising altitude of 4,000 feet. Before long, everyone on board could see the Kent coastline below. A minute or so later, they were flying over the English Channel.

At the rear of the Fokker's cabin there was a windowless door that led into a small toilet. This room also had an exterior door. This door was clearly marked EXIT and was equipped with a spring-loaded latch controlled from inside. It took two strong men to open it in mid-air, due to the slipstream pressing against it.

Loewenstein spent the first half of the flight making notes. Then, as the plane headed out over the Channel, he went to the toilet compartment at the rear.

According to statements later made by Baxter ten minutes

passed and he had still not returned to his seat. Baxter grew concerned and knocked on the toilet door. There was no answer.

Worried that Loewenstein might have been taken ill, he forced open the door. The toilet was empty. Alfred Loewenstein had disappeared into thin air.

An obvious course of action would have been for the plane to divert to the airstrip at St Inglevert, which lay between Calais and Dunkirk. Here, the pilot could have alerted the coastguard to Loewenstein's disappearance. Instead, Donald Drew landed the plane on what he believed to be a deserted beach near Dunkirk.

In actual fact, the beach was being used for training by a local army unit. When the soldiers saw the Fokker coming in to land, they began running along the beach to meet it. It took them six minutes to arrive at the stationary plane, by which time the passengers and crew had disembarked.

They were initially questioned by Lieutenant Marquailles, but he was unable to make any sense of what had happened. Pilot Drew behaved particularly strangely, evading his questions for half an hour until finally admitting that they had lost Alfred Loewenstein somewhere over the English Channel.

Drew was next interrogated by a professional detective named Inspector Bonnot. The inspector confessed to being extremely puzzled by what he was told. 'A most unusual and mysterious case,' he said. 'We have not yet made up our minds to any definite theory, but anything is possible.'

He didn't arrest anyone and even allowed the plane to continue its flight to St Inglevert and then back to Croydon.

The ensuing investigation was bungled from the outset. Loewenstein's body was finally retrieved near Boulogne on 19 July, more than two weeks after his disappearance. It was taken to

Calais by fishing boat where his identity was confirmed by means of his wristwatch.

A post-mortem revealed he had a partial fracture of his skull and several broken bones. Forensic scientists concluded that he had been alive when he hit the water.

The mystery of how he fell to his death remained unanswered, though there are many theories. Some said the absent-minded Loewenstein had accidentally opened the wrong door and fallen to his death. This was most unlikely, given that it was virtually impossible to open the door in mid-flight.

Others said he'd committed suicide, perhaps because his corrupt business practices were about to be exposed.

A far more plausible and sinister explanation is that Loewenstein was forcibly thrown out of the plane by the valet and the male secretary, possibly at the behest of Loewenstein's wife, Madeleine. She had a very frosty relationship with her husband and was desperate to get her hands on his fortune.

One thing is clear: all six people on board were almost certainly privy to the murder. Indeed, they had probably planned it carefully in advance.

One theory as to why the Fokker landed on the beach was so that a new rear door – already stowed on board the plane – could be fitted to replace the one jettisoned over the Channel. This fits neatly with the story of a French fisherman who recalled seeing something like a parachute falling from the sky at precisely the moment Loewenstein went missing. This 'parachute' was quite possibly the rear door.

If the door and Loewenstein were jettisoned over the Channel, it was the perfect crime. No one was ever charged with the murder, nor even directly accused. As for Loewenstein, he was so unpopular that he ended up being laid to rest in an unmarked grave.

Even his 'grieving' widow, Madeleine, didn't show up. She doubtless had more important matters to attend to, organising and investing the fortune that she had just inherited.

PART IX

Not Enough Sex

Castrati: clean cut, penis and testicles severed
Spadones: only testicles amputated
Thlibiae: testicles crushed

THREE TYPES OF CHINESE CASTRATION

25

The Last Eunuch of China

He was just nine years of age when he took the decision that was to transform his life. Sun Yaoting had been chatting with an elderly eunuch who had become rich from serving the Chinese emperor. Soon afterwards, in the autumn of 1911, Sun decided to follow the same path. He asked his father to castrate him in order that he could serve Emperor Puyi, known to history as the 'Last Emperor'.

It was a momentous decision. Unlike eunuchs in the Ottoman Empire, Chinese eunuchs had every bit of their genitals removed. It was an operation that caused not only excruciating pain, but led to a lifetime of sexual frustration, impotence and incontinence.

Sun remained undaunted. On the appointed day, he removed his clothes and lay completely still while his father bound up his hands and feet with rope. Then, with a single violent swoop of a razor, his father performed the operation. In a matter of seconds – and a torrent of blood – Sun had become a eunuch.

He was bandaged with oiled cloth to staunch the bleeding,

but the pain was so agonizing that the young lad lay in a coma for three days. For eight weeks he was virtually paralysed and for months afterwards he was unable to walk because of the excruciating pain. But he eventually recovered from the loss of blood and looked forward to joining the emperor's royal household in the Forbidden City.

Emperor Puyi had more than a thousand eunuchs, many of whom wielded positions of great influence. The emperor rarely left the inner recesses of the palace, meaning that the eunuchs became crucial intermediaries between the outer bureaucratic world and the inner imperial one.

Puyi himself would later write of these 'slaves', who attended him day and night. 'They waited on me when I ate, dressed and slept. They accompanied me on my walks and to my lessons; they told me stories and had rewards and beatings from me, but they never left my presence. They were my slaves and they were my earliest teachers.'

This was the role to which Sun now aspired. He wanted to get the ear of the emperor in order that he might acquire power and influence.

But then came the news that was to leave him in a deep state of shock. The emperor had abdicated, the imperial court was being dismantled and Sun's castration had been in vain.

The dynasty did not die immediately and Sun was not left entirely without hope. He initially found employment with one of the emperor's uncles; later, he worked for Puyi's wife.

In the decades that followed, he was to serve the former imperial family with devotion. He accompanied them to Manchuria, where Puyi was installed as the puppet emperor of the Japanese colonial state of Manchukuo in 1932.

He was also witness to all the innermost secrets of the imperial household, such as the emperor's refusal to sleep with his wife on their wedding night and his obsession with a fellow eunuch, 'who looked like a pretty girl with his tall, slim figure, handsome face and creamy white skin'.

Sun was luckier than the majority of the emperor's eunuchs, who had been abandoned by the court and left penniless. Some became outcasts in society. Many more committed suicide. Others sought sanctuary in the temples of Beijing.

Sun's own life took a downward turn in 1949, when the Communists came to power. Gone were the days when eunuchs were viewed with fear and admiration. Now they were despised as outmoded relics of China's feudal past.

During the Cultural Revolution, Sun lost his most treasured possession, his severed, pickled genitals. Eunuchs always kept them in a jar, in order that they could be buried together. It was believed that such a practice would guarantee their reincarnation as 'whole' men. But Sun's genitals were thrown away like common garbage, causing him to weep openly.

Sun was to live another three decades, dying in 1996 at the age of ninety-four. He never recovered from the loss of his pickled 'treasure'.

'When I die,' he said sadly, 'I will come back as a cat or a dog.'

Further Reading

1. Hitler's English Girlfriend

Litchfield, David R., *Hitler's Valkyrie: The Uncensored Biography of Unity Mitford* (The History Press, 2013).

Lovell, Mary, *The Sisters: The Saga of the Mitford Family* (Norton, 2003).

Pryce-Jones, David, *Unity Mitford: A Quest* (Weidenfeld & Nicholson, 1995).

2. Hitler's American Nephew

Brown, Jonathan & Duff, Oliver, 'The Black Sheep of the Family? The Rise and Fall of Hitler's Scouse Nephew', *Independent*, 17 August 2006: http://www.independent.co.uk/news/uk/this-britain/the-black-sheep-of-the-family-the-rise-and-fall-of-hitlers-scouse-nephew-412206.html

Gardner, David, *The Last of the Hitlers* (BMM, 2001).

Kilgannon, Corey, 'Three Quiet Brothers on Long Island, All of Them Related to Hitler', *New York Times*, 24 April 2006.

3. When Hitler Took Cocaine

Doyle, D., 'Hitler's Medical Care', Royal College of Physicians of Edinburgh, 2005: http://www.ncbi.nlm.nih.gov/pubmed/15825245

Heston, Leonard H., *The Medical Casebook of Adolf Hitler: His Illnesses, Doctors and Drugs* (Cooper Square Publishers, New York, 2000).

Irving, David, *Adolf Hitler: The Secret Diaries of Hitler's Doctor* (Scribner, 1983).

Further Reading

Waite, Robert G. L., *The Psychopathic God: Adolf Hitler* (Da Capo Press, New York, 1993).

4. A Corpse on Everest

Anker, Conrad & Roberts, David, *The Lost Explorer: Finding Mallory on Mount Everest* (Simon & Schuster, 1999).

Davis, Wade, *Into the Silence: The Great War, Mallory and the Conquest of Everest* (Vintage, 2012).

Hemmleb, Jochen, Johnson, Larry A., Simonson, Eric R. & Nothdurft, William E., *Ghosts of Everest: The Search for Mallory & Irvine* (Mountaineers Books, Seattle, 1999).

Hemmleb, Jochen, & Simonson, Eric R., *Detectives on Everest: The Story of the 2001 Mallory & Irvine Research Expedition* (Mountaineers Books, Seattle, 1999).

5. Drunk on the *Titanic*

Encyclopedia Titanica: http://www.encyclopedia-titanica.org/titanic-survivor /charles-john-joughin.html

Lord, Walter, *A Night to Remember* (Transworld, 1955).

Titanic Enquiry Project: http://www.titanicinquiry.org/BOTInq/BOTInq06 Joughin01.php

6. The Man Who Was Buried Alive

Bond, Michael, *The Power of Others* (Oneworld Publications, 2014).

Ice Cap Station: http://www.icecapstation.com/august.html

Scott, Jeremy, *Dancing on Ice: A Stirring Tale of Adventure, Risk and Reckless Folly* (Old Street Publishing Ltd., London, 2008).

7. The Long War of Hiroo Onoda

Kawaguchi, Judith, 'Words to Live By', interview with Hiroo Onoda in *Japan Times*, January 2007.

McFadden, Robert D., 'Hiroo Onoda, Soldier Who Hid in Jungle for Decades, Dies at 91', *New York Times*, 17 January 2014.

Onoda, Hiroo, article and video of interview with 88-year-old Onoda and his wife, filmed in 2010: http://www.abc.net.au/lateline/content/2010/s3065416 .htm

Terry, Charles S., *No Surrender: My Thirty-Year War* (Kodansha International, 1974).

8. The Kamikaze Pilot Who Survived

Allred, Gordon T., & Kuwahara, Yasuo, *Kamikaze: A Japanese Pilot's Own Spectacular Story of the Famous Suicide Squadrons* (Ballantine, 1956).

Hamazono, Shigeyoshi, entry on World War II Database: http://ww2db.com /person_bio.php?person_id=310

McCurry, Justin, 'We were ready to die for Japan', *Guardian*, 2006: http://www .theguardian.com/world/2006/feb/28/worlddispatch.secondworldwar

9. Surviving Hiroshima and Nagasaki

Yamaguchi, Tsutomu, Matsuo, Mari, Sakaoka, Naomi & Brown, Anthony, 'Double A-Bomb Victim: My Life beneath the Atomic Clouds, 2013': http://hdl .handle.net/10069/33740

McCurry, Justin, 'A Little Deaf in One Ear: Meet the Japanese Man who Survived Hiroshima and Nagasaki', *Guardian*, 2009: http://www.theguardian .com/world/2009/mar/25/hiroshima-nagasaki-survivor-japan

McNeill, David, 'How I Survived Hiroshima and then Nagasaki', *Independent*, 2009: http://www.independent.co.uk/news/world/asia/how-i-survived-hiro shima-ndash-and-then-nagasaki-1654294.html

10. Agatha Christie's Greatest Mystery

Christie, Agatha, Official Site: http://www.agathachristie.com/

Morgan, Janet P., *Agatha Christie: A Biography* (Collins, 1984).

Norman, Andrew, *Agatha Christie: The Unfinished Portrait* (History Press, 2007).

Thompson, Laura, *Agatha Christie: An English Mystery* (Headline, 1997).

11. Dressed to Kill

Dorothy Lawrence, *Sapper Dorothy Lawrence: The Only English Woman Soldier, Late Royal Engineers 51st Division 179th Tunnelling Company BEF* (Bodley Head, 1919).

12. Mission into Danger

Halberstam, Yitta & Leventhal, Judith, *Small Miracles of the Holocaust* (Lyons Press, 2008).

Lukas, Richard, *Forgotten Survivors: Polish Christians Remember the Nazi Occupation* (University Press of Kansas, 2004).

Mieszkowska, Anna, *Irena Sendler, Mother of the Children of the Holocaust* (Praeger, 2010).

PBS documentary about Irena Sendler: http://www.pbs.org/program/irena
-sendler/

13. The Real War Horse
Seeley, Jack, *My Horse Warrior* (Hodder & Stoughton, 1934).
Seeley, Jack, *Warrior: The Amazing Story of a Real War Horse* (with an introduction by Jack Seeley's grandson) (Racing Post Books, 2013).
Warrior: A Real War Horse: http://www.warriorwarhorse.com/

14. Pigeon to the Rescue
Cothren, Marion, *Cher Ami: The Story of a Carrier Pigeon* (Little, Brown & Co, 1934).
Laplander, Robert, J., *Finding the Lost Battalion, Beyond the Rumors, Myths and Legends of America's Famous WWI Epic* (Lulu, 2007).
Smithsonian website: http://www.si.edu/Encyclopedia_SI/nmah/cherami.htm

15. Barking for Victory
Bausum, Anne & Sharpe, David E., 'Sergeant Stubby: How a Stray Dog and His Best Friend Helped Win World War I and Stole the Heart of a Nation', *National Geographic*, 2014.
Connecticut Military Department: *Stubby the Military Dog*: http://www.ct.gov/mil/cwp/view.asp?a=1351&q=257892
Smithsonian website: http://historywired.si.edu/detail.cfm?ID=519

16. Angel of Death
Rose, Lionel, *The Massacre of the Innocents* (Routledge, 1986).
Vale, Allison & Rattle, Alison, *Amelia Dyer: Angel Maker* (Andre Deutsch, 2007).

17. Who Killed Rasputin?
Cook, Andrew, *To Kill Rasputin: The Life and Death of Grigori Rasputin* (History Press, 2007).
Milton, Giles, *Russian Roulette* (Sceptre, 2013).
Nelipa, Margarita, *The Murder of Grigorii Rasputin: A Conspiracy That Brought Down the Russian Empire* (Gilbert Books, 2010).
Smith, Michael, *Six* (Biteback, 2010).
Yusupov, Felix, *Lost Splendour: The Amazing Memoirs of the Man Who Killed Rasputin* (Jonathan Cape, 1953).

Further Reading

18. Till Death Us Do Part

Walsh, Cecil, *The Agra Double Murder* (Ernest Benn, 1929).

Whittington-Egan, Molly, *Khaki Mischief: The Agra Murder Case* (Souvenir Press, 1990).

19. By Balloon to the North Pole

PRISM (Polar Radar for Ice Sheet Measurements), 'The Mystery of Andrée', an archive of American newspaper articles 1896–99, with reports about the preparation of the expedition and theories about the explorers' fate: http://ku-prism.org/polarscientist/andreemystery/andreeindex.html

Sollinger, Guenther, *S.A. Andrée: The Beginning of Polar Aviation 1895–1897* (Moscow, 2005).

Wilkinson, Alex, *The Ice Balloon: S. A. Andrée and the Heroic Age of Arctic Exploration* (Fourth Estate, 2012).

20. Escape from Alcatraz

Babyak, Jolene, *Breaking the Rock: The Great Escape from Alcatraz* (Ariel Vamp Press, 2001).

Bruce, Campbell J., *Escape from Alcatraz* (Hammond, 1964).

FBI file on the Alcatraz case: http://vault.fbi.gov/Alcatraz%20Escape

21. A Lonely Trek Through the Andes

Andes Survivors Website: http://www.alpineexpeditions.net/andes-survivors.html

Interviews with Andes Survivors: http://www.viven.com.uy/571/eng/Entrevistas.asp

Parrado, Nando (with Vince Rause), *Miracle in the Andes: 72 Days on the Mountain and My Long Trek Home* (Orion, 2006).

Read, Piers Paul, *Alive: The Story of the Andes Survivors* (Lippincott, Williams & Wilkins, 1974).

22. The First Celebrity Kidnap

Ahlgren, Gregory & Monier, Stephen, *Crime of the Century: The Lindbergh Kidnapping Hoax* (Branden Books, 1993).

Cahill Jr., Richard T., *Hauptmann's Ladder: A Step-by-Step Analysis of the Lindbergh Kidnapping* (Kent State University Press, 2014).

Fisher, Jim, *The Lindbergh Case* (Rutgers University Press, 1994).

FBI case notes on the Lindbergh kidnapping: http://www.fbi.gov/about-us /history/famous-cases/the-lindbergh-kidnapping/the-lindbergh-kidnapping

23. Sir Osman of Hyderabad

Bawa, V.K., *The Last Nizam: The Life and Times of Mir Osman Ali Khan* (Viking, 1991).

Jaisi, Sidq, *The Nocturnal Court: The Life of a Prince of Hyderabad* (Oxford University Press, India, 2004).

Time Magazine, 'His Exalted Highness, The Nizam of Hyderabad', 1937.

24. The Very Strange Death of Alfred Loewenstein

Anon, 'Suicide Hinted in Strange Death of Europe's Croesus', *Evening Independent* (St Petersburg, Florida, 1928).

Norris, William, *The Man Who Fell from the Sky* (Viking, 1987).

Privat, Maurice, *La Vie et la Mort d'Alfred Loewenstein* (La Nouvelle Société d'Edition, 1929).

25. The Last Eunuch of China

Faison, Seth, 'The Death of the Last Emperor's Last Eunuch', *New York Times*, 1996.

Yinghua, Jia & Sun, Haichen (translator), *The Last Eunuch of China: The Life of Sun Yaoting by Jia Yinghua* (China Intercontinental Press, 2008).

BOOK II

When Lenin Lost His Brain

Contents

Part I: When Lenin Lost His Brain

1. When Lenin Lost His Brain   135
2. Into the Monkey House   139
3. The Human Freak Show   143

Part II: Just Bad Luck

4. Freak Wave   149
5. Japan's Deadly Balloon Bomb   154
6. Never Go to Sea   158

Part III: Not Quite Normal

7. Eiffel's Rival   165
8. Emperor of the United States   168
9. The Man Who Bought His Wife   171

Part IV: Mein Führer

10. Hitler's Final Hours   179

Contents

11. Seizing Eichmann   183
12. The Celebrity Executioner   187

Part V: Get Me Out of Here!

13. Trapped on an Iceberg   193
14. Volcano of Death   197
15. The Female Robinson Crusoe   201

Part VI: O What a Lovely War!

16. The Last Post   207
17. To Hell and Back   211
18. Let's Talk Gibberish   215

Part VII: Dial M for Murder

19. Good Ship *Zong*   221
20. The Suspicions of Inspector Dew   225
21. Dead as a Dodo   230

Part VIII: The Great Escape

22. A Sting in the Tale   235
23. And Then There Were None   239
24. Edwin Darling's Nightmare   243

Part IX: A Painful End

25. Never Go to Bed with a Knife   251

Further Reading   *257*

PART I

When Lenin Lost His Brain

Now exhibiting at No. 225 Piccadilly, near the Top of the Haymarket, from twelve 'till four o'clock, Admittance 2s. each, THE HOTTENTOT VENUS, Just arrived from the Interior of Africa, The Greatest Phoenomenon ever Exhibited in this Country, whose stay in the metropolis will be but short.

ADVERTISEMENT FOR SARAH BAARTMAN,
'THE HOTTENTOT VENUS', CIRCA 1810

1

When Lenin Lost His Brain

The mould is regularly wiped from his face and his body is occasionally bathed in glycerol to prevent it from rotting. But despite being on display for almost nine decades, Vladimir Lenin's preserved corpse is in remarkable condition. He looks as if he has drifted into a deep sleep.

But Lenin is hiding a secret, one that is almost invisible to the naked eye. Before being embalmed, scientists sliced open his head and carefully removed his brain in order that it could be studied in microscopic detail. The Soviet regime wanted to know the exact nature of Lenin's genius.

It was an investigation that appalled Lenin's widow, Nadezhda Krupskaya. When her husband died on 21 January 1924, she begged for him to be buried in the plot next to his beloved mother. 'Do not put up buildings or monuments in his name,' she said.

But Lenin's Politburo colleagues strongly disagreed. Indeed, they wanted his corpse to become a permanent monument to the revolution. Felix Dzerzhinsky, chairman of the Lenin Funeral

Committee, said: 'If science permits, Lenin's body must be preserved'.

This posed a real problem. There were many known techniques for embalming a body in the manner of the ancient Egyptians but none that could be guaranteed to preserve Lenin's likeness.

When the distinguished Soviet pathologist Aleksei Abrikosov was asked if it was possible, he replied that 'science today has no such means'. Others disagreed. Vladimir Vorobiev, a professor of anatomy at Kharkov University, argued that 'many anatomical compounds can be preserved for decades; this means we can try and apply them to an entire body'.

The most important organ to be safeguarded was Lenin's brain. It was removed intact from his skull and placed in formaldehyde. For two years, no one dared touch it. But in 1926, the German neurologist Oskar Vogt was invited to try to unlock the key to Lenin's supposed genius. Professor Vogt established the Brain Institute in Moscow, with Lenin's organ as the focus of its studies.

The body had meanwhile been placed in the capable hands of Professor Vorobiev, who was given the weighty responsibility of saving Lenin's flesh from ruin. He was aided in his work by another expert, Boris Zbarsky; both men knew they would be executed if they failed.

Lenin's blood, bodily fluids and internal organs were removed shortly after the brain, as part of the initial embalming process. (The whereabouts of his heart remains a mystery to this day; it seems to have been lost shortly afterwards.)

Once the internal organs had been removed, the corpse was immersed for many weeks in a special solution that contained glycerol and acetate. The dark, mould-like spots that had started to appear on the body were later removed with acetic acid and hydrogen peroxide.

It was essential to keep the eye sockets from collapsing: artificial eyes were inserted into the holes as replacements for the originals. It was also important that the face looked as lifelike as possible. Lenin's eyebrows, moustache and goatee were therefore left untouched. His genitals, too, were left in situ (although it goes without saying that they're not on display).

While the body underwent a lengthy embalming process, the brain was given a detailed examination. Professor Vogt had long argued that there was a direct link between brain structure and intelligence. If correct in this assumption, there was no reason why he couldn't map the origins of Lenin's supposed genius.

The professor chopped the brain into four chunks and then had each chunk sliced into 7,500 microscopically thin sections. This required a custom-built brain slicer, not unlike the slicing machines used to cut Parma ham.

Some slices were stained purple and black for study under microscopes. The rest were left untouched in order that future generations might be able to study them.

Vogt and his team of Soviet scientists spent years studying the slices of brain and trying to make sense of their findings. The results of their scientific tests were eventually set down in fourteen volumes bound in green leather and embossed with a single word: LENIN.

But neither the professor's work, nor that of the scientists that followed in his wake, was ever published. It was not until 1993 that Dr Oleg Adrianov, one of the Brain Institute's most distinguished technicians, was finally allowed to publish a paper on Lenin's brain.

There was good reason why the findings could not be made

public earlier. Lenin's brain did indeed hold a secret, one so shocking that the Soviet hierarchy was determined to keep it under wraps.

The secret was this: his brain was no different from that of anyone else. 'A brain is like a water melon,' said Dr Adrianov, 'ninety-five per cent of it is liquid.' Although Lenin's brain had unusually large pyramidal neurons, this had no reflection on its internal mechanism. 'Frankly,' said Dr Adrianov, 'I do not think he was a genius.'

And what of the rest of his body? For many years his corpse was under the supervision of Yuri Denisov-Nikolsky. When asked about his macabre job, he confessed to having shaking hands whenever he touched it.

'Not every expert is allowed to restore such treasured historical objects, like a Raphael or a Rembrandt. Those who do it, we tremble. I feel a great responsibility in my hands.'

Boris Yeltsin was the first senior political leader to suggest that Lenin should be buried. He said that following the collapse of the Soviet Union it was no longer appropriate to keep his corpse on show.

But neither he, nor Vladimir Putin, nor any other senior politician has been inclined to remove from display what must surely rank as one of the most macabre tourist attractions in the world.

So there he lies, marble white, wrinkled and sometimes a little mouldy. His brain, meanwhile, is being held in storage a mile or so across town, sliced into 30,000 slivers mounted on glass slides. No one has yet proposed that body and brain should be reunited.

2

Into the Monkey House

The Bronx Zoo in New York attracted large crowds of visitors whenever newly acquired animals were first put on display. In previous years, it was the elephants and lions that had been the crowd-pullers. Tigers, too, proved extremely popular.

But in September 1906, the zoo's new addition was altogether more alluring. Ota Benga was a pygmy from the African Congo and he had been locked up in the monkey house.

Ota Benga had been brought to New York by an American businessman-cum-missionary named Samuel Phillips Verner. Verner had travelled to the Belgian Congo in 1904 in order to acquire an assortment of African pygmies for display at the St Louis World Fair.

Verner first met Ota Benga while on an expedition deep into the equatorial rainforest. He managed to barter him for a pound of salt and a roll of cloth. Ota Benga was unwilling to leave Africa on his own and managed to persuade a few companions to join him on an expedition to North America. It was a voyage that was to change their lives.

Ota Benga proved an instant (if controversial) attraction at the world fair. He was put on display with other pygmies in the fair's anthropology tent.

Part of the attraction was his strange teeth; they had been filed to sharp points when he was a young boy, as part of a Congolese ritualistic ceremony. Newspapers described him as 'the only genuine African cannibal in America'.

Ota Benga returned briefly to the Congo after the fair but made a second visit to America with Verner in 1906. This time, his treatment was far more injurious. After a brief spell at the American Museum of Natural History, he was moved to Bronx Zoo.

The zoo's director, William Hornaday, was quick to realize the appeal of a 'human savage' on display. Aware that it was controversial, he sought the backing of Madison Grant, the distinguished secretary of the New York Zoological Society.

Grant thought that it was a brilliant idea; Ota Benga was to live in the monkey house, along with a parrot and an orangutan called Dahong. The display panel read: 'The African Pygmy, Ota Benga. Age, 23 years. Height, 4 feet 11 inches. Weight, 103 pounds. Brought from the Kasai River, Congo Free State, South Central Africa, by Dr. Samuel P. Verner. Exhibited each afternoon during September.'

In an article for the Zoological Society's bulletin, Hornaday wrote enthusiastically about the zoo's new acquisition: 'A *genuine* African Pygmy, belonging to the sub-race commonly miscalled "the dwarfs". Ota Benga is a well-developed little man, with a good head, bright eyes and a pleasing countenance. He is not hairy, and is not covered by the "downy felt" described by some explorers.'

His presence in the zoo excited controversy from the opening day. Indeed, it was to spark a violent debate about racism, evolution and evolutionary Darwinism.

The *New York Times* initially defended the decision to put him in the monkey house. 'We do not quite understand all the emotion which others are expressing in the matter,' declared their editorial. 'It is absurd to make moan over the imagined humiliation and degradation Benga is suffering. The pygmies are very low in the human scale, and the suggestion that Benga should be in a school instead of a cage ignores the high probability that school would be a place from which he could draw no advantage whatever.'

The debate intensified with every day that passed. White churchmen were dismayed by Ota Benga's presence in the monkey cage, not because it was inhumane but because they felt he was being used to promote Darwin's theory of evolution. This was something that many of them opposed.

African American churchmen were even more appalled by Ota Benga's new home. Pastor James Gordon spoke for many when he said that 'our race, we think, is depressed enough, without exhibiting one of us with the apes. We think we are worthy of being considered human beings, with souls'.

Before long, Ota Benga was released from the monkey house and allowed to wander freely around the zoo dressed in a white linen suit. But this scarcely helped his plight.

Visitors taunted him and tried to poke and prod him. According to William Hornaday, 'he procured a carving knife from the feeding room of the Monkey House and went around the Park flourishing it in a most alarming manner'.

The *New York Times* now changed its tune and joined the growing chorus of dissent about Ota Benga's treatment. The newspaper complained that his time at the zoo had only served to brutalize him. At the end of 1906, he was released from captivity and housed in an orphan asylum in New York.

Ota Benga always dreamed of returning to Africa but it was not to be. When the First World War broke out – and the Atlantic crossing became too dangerous – he despaired of ever making it back to the Congo. Depressed by his experience of life in the 'land of the free', he stole a pistol and shot himself through the heart. He was buried in an unmarked grave in New York.

The American Museum of Natural History retains a life-size cast of Ota Benga's head and shoulders. To this day it is not marked with his name or any indication that he was a human being. The label has just one word: 'pygmy'.

3

The Human Freak Show

She was forced to squat in front of a jeering mob, a bewildered stranger who was far from home. The crowd stared at her protruding buttocks and oversized vulva before cracking lewd and bawdy jokes.

Sarah Baartman had arrived in England a few weeks earlier, in the autumn of 1810, and had already earned herself unwitting notoriety as the 'Hottentot Venus'. Now, she was displayed (to a fee-paying audience) as a sexual deviant and an example of the inferiority of the black race.

Baartman had been brought to England from Cape Town by a British doctor named William Dunlop. He was fascinated by her large buttocks and genitalia – a common trait in the Khoisan people to whom she belonged – and realized that she had the potential to earn him lots of money. He coerced her into travelling to London with the promise that she would get very rich.

Sarah Baartman's arrival in the capital came less than three years after the abolition of the slave trade. She was taken to fashionable Piccadilly where, outside number 225, she was exposed to the city's baying crowds.

According to a contemporary account, she was paraded on a two-foot high stage 'along which she was led by her keeper and exhibited like a wild beast, being obliged to walk, stand or sit as he ordered'.

Her promoters had originally intended her to be completely naked, but this proved too risqué. Instead, she was 'dressed in a colour as nearly resembling her skin as possible'. According to *The Times*, 'the dress is contrived to exhibit the entire frame of her body, and the spectators are even invited to examine the peculiarities of her form'. The show's promoters knew what the punters were paying to see: they billed Sarah's genitals as resembling the skin that hangs from a turkey's throat.

The spectacle of an enslaved woman being put on public display courted controversy from the outset. Among the outraged was a young Jamaican named Robert Wedderburn. He knew all too well the horrors of slavery, for his mother had been the slave of a Scottish sugar plantation owner. When she had fallen pregnant, Wedderburn senior had sold her to an aristocrat friend with the proviso that the baby should be free from birth.

Robert's rough upbringing left him with a strong sense of justice. He was appalled by the spectacle of Sarah Baartman being paraded before the crowds. After courting the abolitionist African Association, he petitioned for her release.

In November 1810, the attorney general tried to discover whether 'she was exhibited by her own consent'. Two affidavits were produced which suggested that she had never agreed to be brought to England for public display.

The first affidavit revealed that she had been brought to Britain by people who referred to her as their private property. The second described the degrading conditions under which she was exhibited.

Sarah herself was also questioned. She claimed that she had not been coerced and had been promised half the profits of her travelling tour. But her testimony was flawed and was almost certainly made under coercion.

The attorney general backed the attempt to stop the freak show, but the court ruled that Sarah had entered into a contract of her own free will. The show went on.

After four years on the road, Sarah was moved to Paris where she was sold to a travelling circus. Her promoters made extra money by exhibiting her at society functions where she proved an instant hit with the guests.

At one ball she was dressed in nothing but a few feathers; Napoleon's surgeon general, George Cuvier, was fascinated by the sight and began a detailed study of her body.

Sarah eventually turned to alcohol and prostitution and died in 1815, possibly of syphilis. Cuvier managed to acquire her corpse, which he promptly dissected. He then pickled Sarah's genitals and brain, and put them on display, along with her skeleton.

She remained in the Musée de l'Homme until 1974, when public revulsion caused the pickled body parts to be removed. But it was not until 2002, after the intervention of Nelson Mandela, that her remains were finally returned to her native South Africa and given a decent burial.

Sarah was neither the first nor last person to be displayed as a human freak. Seventy years later, another human specimen found himself being paraded through the streets of London. His name was Joseph Merrick, better known as the Elephant Man.

His skeleton is yet to be buried: it is still housed in the pathology collection of the Royal London Hospital.

PART II

Just Bad Luck

It was just like a mountain, a wall of water
coming against us . . .
I had to swim and crawl to get back to the controls
to put the ship back on course.

GÖRAN PERSSON, FIRST OFFICER ON THE
CALEDONIAN STAR WHEN THE SHIP WAS HIT BY
A 90-FOOT FREAK WAVE.

4

Freak Wave

On Boxing Day 1900, the Scottish supply ship SS *Hesperus* dropped anchor close to the Flannan Isles, a windswept group of islands near Scotland's Outer Hebrides. The vessel had come to deliver essential supplies to the three lighthouse keepers who had been left on the island some three weeks earlier.

The *Hesperus*'s crew were expecting the usual welcome: two of the keepers normally rowed out to greet the arriving vessel while the third raised a flag as a sign that all was well. But on this occasion, there was no sign of any rowing boat and no raising of the flag. Captain Harvie gave a blast on the ship's siren and awaited a response. There was none.

More intrigued than alarmed, he ordered two of his crew – Joseph Moore and Second Mate McCormack – to row ashore in the ship's boat.

When the men landed at the island they shouted greetings to the keepers. There was no reply. All they heard was the echo of their own voices. As they made their way towards the lighthouse, they grew increasingly concerned. There was no sign of any life and the lighthouse's outer door was locked.

Moore had a set of keys and now proceeded to unlock the building. With trepidation he pushed the creaking door and stepped inside. Silence. He called the men's names. There was no one. James Ducat, Thomas Marshall and Donald Macarthur had mysteriously disappeared.

Moore looked around and took a mental note of everything he saw. The clock on the inner wall had stopped working. There was no fire in the grate and the three beds were empty. A meal had been left uneaten on the table. It was as if the men had been spirited away.

The three keepers had been ferried to the Flannan Isles on 7 December 1900. They had been accompanied by Robert Muirhead, the Superintendent of Lighthouses, who wanted to make a routine inspection of the building and check that the place was well supplied.

This was important, for the Flannan Isles were one of the loneliest spots on earth. They stand some twenty miles to the west of the Outer Hebrides, a place so forlorn that the rotating lighthouse crews were rarely left for more than a few weeks. Longer stays on the island had been known to drive men mad.

Once he was satisfied that all was well, Robert Muirhead had helped the three outgoing keepers onto his ship, wished the new team luck and then bade them farewell. He was the last person to see them alive.

In the week that followed Muirhead's departure, the island was kept under close telescopic observation from the Outer Hebrides. It had long been arranged that if an emergency arose, the keepers were to hoist a large flag. A boat would then be sent to the island to bring help.

It was a system that worked, but imperfectly. The island was often obscured by banks of swirling sea mist, and the distance from the Outer Hebrides was such that it meant accurate observation was almost impossible.

For several days that followed the arrival of James Ducat and his team, the island was enveloped in thick fog and the lighthouse was invisible for much of that time.

The lamp itself was easier to see, especially at night. It was glimpsed on the evening of 7 December, a sign that all was well, but then obscured by bad weather for the next four evenings. It was sighted again on 12 December. After that, it was not seen again.

Three days after the last sighting, a vessel named the SS *Archtor* passed close to the island. Captain Holman looked for the light in the night sky but saw nothing. He was concerned that something was wrong and immediately raised the alarm.

Atrocious weather prevented the SS *Hesperus* from reaching the island until Boxing Day, when Moore and McCormack finally managed to row ashore. When they found the lighthouse to be empty, they searched the rocky island for the three keepers. They were nowhere to be seen.

Moore and McCormack rowed back to the *Hesperus* in order to inform Captain Harvie of the men's mysterious disappearance. The captain, in turn, signalled the mystery to the Northern Lighthouse Board.

'A dreadful accident has happened at the Flannan,' he wrote. 'The three keepers, Ducat, Marshall and the Occasional [Macarthur] have disappeared from the island. Poor fellows must have been blown over the cliffs or drowned trying to secure a crane or something like that.'

An investigation was soon under way, led by Superintendent

Muirhead. After a detailed search of both the lighthouse and island, he was able to piece together a story of what might have happened to the men. It was one that few were prepared to believe.

Muirhead was confident that everything had been running smoothly until the afternoon of 15 December. The principal lighthouse keeper, James Ducat, had compiled weather reports until the 13th, and had also written draft entries for 14 and 15 December. These revealed that there had been a storm on 14 December, followed by a surprising calm on the next morning. After that, there were no more entries. In the aftermath of that calm, something had gone seriously, fatally wrong.

Muirhead's inspection of the island proved most revealing. He found that the lighthouse and its outbuildings had sustained considerable damage, to the extent that some of these buildings had been structurally weakened. The jetty was badly warped and the iron railings had been strangely contorted, as if a giant fist had wrenched them apart. One of the storehouses, built to withstand winter storms, had been washed clean away.

When Muirheard examined the upper levels of the lighthouse, he found something so bizarre that it was almost impossible to explain. The lighthouse ropes, usually stored at ground level, had become snared on a crane that stood 70 feet above sea level.

Muirhead could only offer two hypotheses as to what might have happened and neither seemed particularly plausible. Either the three men had been blown off the cliffs – a conjecture that did nothing to explain the snared ropes – or they had been swept off the island by what Muirhead referred to as 'an extra large sea'. What he meant, but declined to say for fear of ridicule, was a gigantic freak wave.

Few people countenanced such an idea at the time of the disaster. Freak waves were believed to exist only in novels, poems and sailors' fertile imaginations. It was deemed impossible that Muirhead's 'extra large sea' could have swept the men to their deaths.

But it is now known that freak waves (not to be confused with tsunami or tidal waves) do exist and can be immensely destructive. In 2001, the expedition ship *Caledonian Star* was hit by a 90-foot wall of water that seemed to arise from nowhere. It struck the ship with such force that the bridge windows were shattered and the ship's electricity wiped out. The crews of other vessels have described similarly destructive waves. They are caused by the conjunction of high winds and strong currents that produce an underwater surge. Given the right atmospheric conditions, this can be forced upwards to create a truly violent natural phenomenon.

It will never be known for certain what happened to the unfortunate men on the Flannan Isles. But it seems likely that they were swept off their rocky home by a huge wave – at least 70 feet in height – that then sucked them into the undertow and carried them to a watery grave.

5

Japan's Deadly Balloon Bomb

Pastor Archie Mitchell had promised his wife, Elsie, a treat. Both of them were tired of reading newspaper articles about the war in the Far East. On Saturday 5 May 1945, Archie suggested a day of escapism, driving up into the mountains of southern Oregon and having a picnic.

Elsie was delighted by the prospect and even happier when Archie offered to bring along five children from their local church. Elsie was heavily pregnant and the idea of taking the youngsters on a special outing had a particular appeal.

They set off by car in late morning and were soon winding through spectacular mountain scenery. The children were restless in the crowded car and wanted to hike across the hills. Archie suggested that Elsie lead them on foot to Leonard Creek, a well-known beauty spot, while he drove round in the car. It would enable him to start preparing the lunch.

The children were delighted and waved their goodbyes before setting off into the forest. Archie meanwhile drove to Leonard Creek and began installing the picnic.

It was while he was unpacking the sandwiches that he heard shouts from a couple of the children. Breathless with excitement, they said they had found a strange balloon lying on the ground just a short distance away.

Archie warned them not to touch it in case it was dangerous. He promised to come and inspect the balloon just as soon as he had finished preparing the picnic.

As he was setting off to see what they had found, the ground beneath him was suddenly rocked by a tremendous explosion. A series of shockwaves ripped through the undergrowth, filling the air with dust. A plume of black smoke could be seen rising above the trees.

Archie rushed to the scene, only to find the trees shredded and charred. But worse, far worse, was the fact that twenty-six-year-old Elsie, together with the five children, Dick Patzke, fourteen, Jay Gifford, Edward Engen and Joan Patzke, all thirteen, and Sherman Shoemaker, eleven, were sprawled on the ground and covered in blood. On closer inspection – and to his absolute horror – he saw that all of them were dead.

He had no idea what had happened and could only assume that the 'strange balloon' had somehow exploded. Only later did he discover that Elsie and the children had been the victims of a balloon bomb, a devastating new weapon that the Japanese were intending to drop on North America in massive quantities.

This Japanese bomb represented a terrible new threat. Unpredictable and highly explosive, it also had the potential to disperse biological agents across the length and breath of the country.

It was the brainchild of Major General Sueyoshi Kusaba, head of the Japanese Army's secret Number Nine Research Laboratory. The technical work was supervised by a gifted scientist by the name of Major Taiji Takada.

Their idea was strikingly simple: to use the winter jet stream to carry bomb-laden balloons from Japan to North America, where they would land and explode, causing widespread destruction. Better still, from the Japanese point of view, they would instil fear into the American population at large.

Research revealed that the jet stream could carry a large balloon at high altitude across the 5,000 miles of Pacific Ocean in about three days. But there were some technical hurdles to be overcome if the balloons were to be successful.

The most pressing problem was the fact that they were filled with hydrogen, which expanded in the warmth of the sunshine and contracted in the cool of night. To prevent this from happening, the balloon had to be fitted with special altimeters programmed to jettison ballast if the balloon descended too low. Once the prototypes had been successfully tested, the balloon project got under way in earnest.

There was enormous potential for destruction. Each balloon carried a massive incendiary bomb as well as high-explosive devices that could target cities and (in the dry heat of midsummer) forests.

In the first week of November 1944 the first wave of bombs was launched. Chief scientist Takada was there for the lift-off. 'The figure of the balloon was visible only for several minutes following its release,' he later recalled, 'until it faded away as a spot in the blue sky like a daytime star.'

The initial wave of balloons landed and exploded in no fewer than seventeen states, as far apart as Alaska, Texas, Michigan and California.

General Kusaba was hoping that 10 per cent of his balloons would reach their target destination: with more than 9,000 on the production line, this represented a significant threat to the United States.

America soon awoke to the dangers of this devastating new weapon, which struck at random and without warning. Fighter jets were scrambled to intercept the balloons but they met with little success. Japan's wonder-weapon flew extremely high and fast and fewer than twenty were shot down from the sky.

Balloons soon started landing and exploding right across America. News of their existence was kept secret: the Office of Censorship ordered newspapers not to mention the bombings lest they create widespread panic.

Japan was meanwhile reporting massive damage to American property. One article claimed as many as 10,000 casualties in a single raid.

In truth, the balloons proved less effective than the Japanese had hoped. Nor were they particularly accurate: the vast majority landed on farmland or in the sea.

Japan's scientists worked tirelessly to increase the accuracy of the bombs and they also developed biological and chemical weapons that could be attached to the balloons and dropped onto American cities.

Given time, they might well have proved successful. But all the major technological breakthroughs came too late. The war was almost at an end and Japan was itself about to be the target of a devastating new weapon. The only known fatalities of the Japanese balloon bombings were Elsie Mitchell and her picnic party of five schoolchildren.

Archie's life was ruined by what had happened: he had lost his wife, his unborn baby and his young parishioners. But his woes were not yet at an end. In 1960, while serving as a missionary in Vietnam, he was captured by the Viet Cong.

He disappeared without trace and was never seen again.

6

Never Go to Sea

On a sparkling winter's day in 1826, a young Englishwoman named Ann Saunders boarded a vessel that was sailing from New Brunswick in Canada to Liverpool.

She was looking forward to the Atlantic voyage: the outward journey had been a delight and the return seemed set to be the same. 'We set sail', she later wrote, 'with a favourable wind and the prospect and joyful expectations of an expeditious passage.'

There were twenty-one people on board, including Ann's close friend Mrs Kendall, the wife of the captain.

The *Francis Mary* had been at sea for almost three weeks when, on the first day of February, she was hit by a ferocious storm. 'About noon, our vessel was struck by a tremendous sea, which swept from her decks almost every moveable object.' Ann watched on helpless as one of the mariners was washed overboard. He was extremely fortunate to be saved from the water by his comrades.

Worse was to come. As the storm increased in intensity, it lashed at the timbers and pitched the vessel from peak to trough.

Ann watched in terror as a monstrous wave emerged from no-where, slamming against the side of the vessel and striking with such force that it ripped away a part of the hull.

Water gushed into the hold, flooding the storage areas and threatening to drag the ship down. The *Francis Mary* was already listing heavily when another huge wave struck the vessel and flipped her upwards through forty-five degrees. Everyone on board clung to the rigging and slowly pulled themselves up towards the forecastle, the only part of the ship that remained above the waterline.

Still she didn't sink. Indeed, she had stabilized at an erratic angle in the water, heaving up and down in the heavy swell.

Several of the crew now made a desperate attempt to descend into the waterlogged interior and rescue whatever provisions they could. At great risk to their lives they clambered below decks and managed to drag out 50 pounds of bread and biscuit, along with a few pounds of cheese. It was precious little sustenance for everyone on board, especially as they were exposed to the full fury of an Atlantic winter.

It was not long before they began to die. James Clarke was the first to succumb: he breathed his last on 12 February and his body was hurled overboard.

Next to die was John Wilson. His death coincided with the last of the biscuit rations being consumed. After a brisk debate, the crew and passengers took the momentous decision to keep themselves alive by eating him.

Ann Saunders watched on stoically as Wilson's corpse was roughly dismembered and then chopped into manageable chunks. 'It was cut into slices, then washed in salt water, and after being exposed to and dried a little in the sun, was apportioned to each of the miserable survivors.'

Ann was of a genteel disposition and could not bring herself to eat human flesh. She refused to take her portion. But after twenty-four hours of further starvation she 'was compelled by hunger to follow their example'.

She noticed that the group act of cannibalism changed the dynamics of life aboard the stricken vessel. 'We eyed each other with mournful and melancholy looks,' she said. Each person had become a potential meal.

Men now began to die every day. When Sailor Moore succumbed to exposure they feasted on his liver and heart. Henry David and John Jones were the next to expire, followed by several of the cabin boys. One of them died 'raving mad, crying out lamentably'. All were dismembered and consumed by the surviving crew.

Several barrels of water had been rescued in the aftermath of the storm. These now ran dry, obliging those on board to 'the melancholy distressful horrid act (to procure of their blood) of cutting the throats of their deceased companions a moment after the breath of life had left their bodies'.

Miss Saunders watched aghast as her female companion Mrs Kendall munched through the brains of one of the seamen. When the last morsel was finished, she turned to the others with dripping fingers and declared it 'the most delicious thing she ever tasted'.

The next death weighed particularly heavily on young Ann. James Frier was a youthful admirer of hers, one who had plucked up the courage to propose marriage in the terrible days that followed the storm. Ann had accepted without hesitation and promised to tie the knot as soon as they reached England.

Now, as young James slipped from unconsciousness into death, she had little choice but to eat him. She described herself as being 'so far reduced by hunger and thirst' that she was obliged 'to suck the blood as it oozed half-congealed from the wound inflicted upon his lifeless body'.

Several more of the crew expired in the days that followed Frier's death and soon there were only six people left alive. When a vessel was finally sighted on the horizon – it was the HMS *Blonde* – all six were on the verge of death.

The captain of the *Blonde* was horrified to discover that those aboard the *Francis Mary* had kept themselves alive by gorging on their crewmates. He was even more appalled to discover that the ship's ropes were adorned with thin slices of human flesh left to dry in the stiff sea breeze. Yet he took pity on the gaunt survivors and rescued them from their waterlogged vessel.

The *Blonde* finally arrived in England in April 1826 with Ann and five others. Although deeply shaken by her ordeal, Ann was relieved to have survived a voyage that had killed fifteen of her travelling companions. And she remained surprisingly philosophical about having eaten her fiancé.

'I think that I witnessed more of the heavy judgements and afflictions of this world than any other of its female inhabitants,' she said.

PART III

Not Quite Normal

We, Norton I, by the Grace of God Emperor of the Thirty-three states and the multitude of Territories of the United States of America, do hereby dissolve the Republic of the United States.

EMPEROR NORTON'S 1860 DECREE DISSOLVING THE
UNITED STATES GOVERNMENT AND REPLACING
IT WITH AN ABSOLUTE MONARCHY.

7

Eiffel's Rival

It was the crowning achievement of his career. Gustav Eiffel was feted as a French national hero at the 1889 inauguration of his famous tower.

Among the few who did not appreciate his Paris skyscraper was a fervent English patriot by the name of Edward Watkin. He resented the Eiffel Tower for one simple reason: it stood more than five times higher than Britain's most celebrated monument, Nelson's Column. And that, he felt, was a deep insult to national pride.

Yet Watkin was not a man to nurse his grievances. He vowed to do everything in his power to construct a British tower that would be taller, bigger and more spectacular than anything the French could build.

Watkin had made his fortune in railways, building extensive networks in England, India and the Belgian Congo. Immensely energetic and ambitious, he was always looking for ways to increase his fortune.

He reasoned that if his planned mega-tower was built in Wembley Park, a stretch of unused wasteland in the north-west of London, then his own Metropolitan Railway could be used to transport the thousands of annual visitors that would surely flock to the site.

Watkin was convinced that he was onto a winning idea and now launched his competition to build a British tower – one that would overshadow Gustav Eiffel's monument. 'Anything Paris can do, London can do better!' was his war cry.

By the end of 1889, architects from across the world were working on designs for a tower that would be taller and more spectacular than Eiffel's. There was to be a prize of 500 guineas for the best-designed entry.

The project fired the public imagination and gained a great deal of publicity. Watkin's Metropolitan Tower Construction Company became a byword for national pride. With more than a hint of mischief, Watkin even approached Gustav Eiffel and asked if he would care to submit an entry.

Eiffel politely declined. 'If I,' he said, 'after erecting my tower on French soil, were to erect one in England, they would not think me so good a Frenchman as I hope I am.'

It was not long before a variety of designs began to arrive on Watkin's desk: they came from Italy, Sweden and Turkey, along with many local ones.

Watkin was disappointed to discover that many of them were eccentric flights of fancy. One, named Ye Vegetarian Tower, was submitted by the London Vegetarian Society. It came complete with hanging vegetable gardens. Another, the so-called Tower of Babel, was so vast that it had a road and railway leading to the top. The most extraordinary design of all – a tower far taller than Eiffel's – was to be built entirely of glass.

As Edward Watkin leafed through the numerous entries, he realized there was only one design that stood any practical chance of being built. It was made of open metal latticework and rose to a point at the top. Standing upon four legs (the original design had six) it was in every respect an exact copy of the Eiffel Tower. The only difference was that it was 87 feet taller.

It was selected as the winning entry and building work began immediately. By 1891, the gigantic foundation holes in Wembley Park had been plugged with concrete and work began on the 3,000-ton tower itself.

Work began well. It had soon reached a height of more than 60 feet and curious Londoners began to flock to see the beginnings of what was being called Watkin's Tower.

Edward Watkin claimed it would be finished by 1894. But this proved wildly optimistic. When the surrounding park was opened to the public in that year, the tower was still only 155 feet high.

Some 100,000 people came to visit the stump. Most were extremely disappointed to see a partial replica of Eiffel's architectural triumph. Only 18,500 bothered to buy a ticket to ascend to the first (and only) level.

At the end of 1894, Edward Watkin's workmen downed their tools. The Metropolitan Tower Construction Company had run out of money and the general public no longer had any enthusiasm for a project that seemed increasingly pointless.

The tower was abandoned shortly afterwards. For the next thirteen years, Watkin's folly remained as an embarrassment on the London skyline, a rusting and derelict eyesore.

By the time it was finally blown up in 1907, Edward Watkin was dead and Britain had signed the Entente Cordiale with France. Anglo-French rivalry was set aside – for the time being.

8

Emperor of the United States

He reigned for more than two decades, an autocratic monarch with absolute powers over one of the most powerful countries on earth. Emperor Joshua Norton I declared himself supreme ruler of the United States in 1859: his avowed intention was to restore stability and integrity to a country he felt was falling into ruin.

Emperor Norton might easily have been dismissed as a harmless eccentric, were it not for the fact that he had a large number of supporters. Promoted by the newspapers of San Francisco, his decrees and proclamations soon became known across the entire nation.

His reign began on 17 September 1859, when he issued a proclamation to the Californian papers: 'I declare and proclaim myself emperor of these United States.' He immediately called for a public meeting of representatives of all the different states in America, signing his declaration: *Norton I, Emperor of the United States*. (He soon added *Protector of Mexico* to his title.)

The proclamation was greeted with wild enthusiasm by the people of California. They loved his conviction, his authority and his bluntly worded decrees. Norton's clever manipulation of the media rapidly turned him into a nationwide celebrity.

He achieved even greater publicity when he awarded himself autocratic powers. With a theatrical flourish, he formally abolished the House of Congress in the second week of October 1859.

'Open violation of the laws are constantly occurring,' he declared, 'caused by mobs, parties, factions and undue influence of political sects. The citizen has not that protection of person and property to which he is entitled.'

The following year, Emperor Norton called upon the army to forcibly depose the elected members of Congress, in order that he might consolidate his tenuous grip on power.

The army and congress chose to ignore Norton, but he was not disheartened. In 1862, he ordered the Protestant and Roman Catholic churches to ordain him emperor. (They also ignored him.) Seven years later, he abolished the Democratic and Republican parties. Shortly afterwards, he issued a decree forbidding religious warfare.

Norton was a familiar figure in his imperial capital of San Francisco. He wore a navy military uniform with gold epaulettes and a spectacular beaver-skin hat bedecked with rosettes and peacock feathers. Twirling a cane in his hand, he liked to patrol the streets, chatting with his subjects and inspecting the state of public buildings.

He had been a penniless bankrupt in the years before proclaiming himself emperor. It was his flair for showmanship that had rescued him from ruin. Dressed in his unmistakable regalia, he was invited to dine in San Francisco's finest restaurants.

In return for free food, he would reward them with an imperial seal: 'By appointment to his Imperial Majesty, Emperor Norton I of the United States.'

Restaurants fought to get such seals as they provided a significant boost to trade. The emperor was also much sought after by theatres and music halls and always had the best seat reserved for him on opening nights.

He had his occasional brush with the law, but usually got the upper hand. When he was arrested and committed to a mental asylum in 1867, there was a public outcry. It led to his immediate release and a grovelling apology from the police. Ever magnanimous, Norton granted an imperial pardon to the officers who arrested him.

By the 1870s, Norton was issuing his own currency: the banknotes became widely accepted in San Francisco. He was also granted recognition of sorts by the United States government: the 1870 census lists his occupation as 'emperor'.

His reign was to last another decade before coming to a dramatic end: in January 1880, he collapsed in the street and was pronounced dead shortly afterwards.

The *San Francisco Chronicle* announced the tragic news to the world. Under a banner headline in French, 'Le Roi est Mort', it said: 'In the darkness of a moonless night under the dripping rain, Norton I, by the grace of God, Emperor of the United States and Protector of Mexico, departed this life.'

He was buried in Woodlawn Cemetery in California and was given a headstone that still draws the eye of curious visitors: 'Norton I, Emperor of the United States and Protector of Mexico'.

9

The Man Who Bought His Wife

S amuel Baker had always enjoyed the thrill of the hunt: it offered excitement, adventure and the chance to spend time in the great outdoors. When he was asked to accompany Duleep Singh, the crowned ruler of the Punjab, on a hunting trip around central Europe, he jumped at the opportunity. It was a trip that would bag him a most unusual quarry.

The journey had begun conventionally enough. The two men had shot their way through large numbers of birds, bears and wolves. But their progress through the hunting grounds hit a snag in January 1859, when their wooden boat was damaged by an ice floe in the River Danube. They had little option but to take a temporary break from hunting while the craft was repaired.

The riverside town in which they found themselves was called Vidin, a provincial town in Bulgaria, then a province of the Ottoman Empire. It was a dreary place to put ashore: there were no particular sights and little to occupy the two men. The impatient maharajah was keen for some entertainment.

Samuel Baker soon found something to keep his Punjabi host

amused. He learned that the Finjanjian family, the town's most important dealers in white slaves, was about to hold an auction. The matriarch of the family was selling off some of the harem girls.

Among the slaves for sale was Florenz Szasz, a beautiful teenager from Transylvania. Although young, she had already undergone more adventures than most people experience in a lifetime. Orphaned in the 1848 Hungarian Revolution when still a young girl, she had endured both adoption and abduction. She had eventually ended up in the Finjanjian family's harem.

Now, in January 1859, her life was about to take an entirely new twist. She was to be sold at auction, with her future in the hands of the highest bidder.

In the days before the auction, Florenz was prepared for the market. She was given new clothes that accentuated her comely figure and an advertisement about her forthcoming sale was placed in local newspapers.

As a virgin, she almost certainly had a certificate of virginity signed by a certified midwife: proof of virginity greatly enhanced the value of female slaves.

Astonishingly, Florenz did not know she was being sold until the day of the auction. Only when she saw the potential buyers gathered in the opulent public salon of the Finjanjian mansion did she realize what was taking place.

Most of the slave buyers were wealthy Ottoman Turks. But as Florenz scanned the room, she saw one face that was clearly not Turkish. Samuel Baker had curly russet hair, thick sideburns and wore a wool tweed suit. He was instant recognizable as being English. His companion was equally recognizable as being Indian.

Baker was not attending the slave sale with the intention of buying anyone: he had a moral abhorrence of slavery that was to endure throughout his life. He was attending solely because he thought it would be an entertaining diversion for the maharajah.

But he was deeply affected when the young Florenz was brought out for public display. She was beautiful, vulnerable and seemingly terrified of being sold to a Turkish master. Baker found himself shaken to the core. His own wife had died four years earlier, now, desperate to save the young girl, he placed a bid for her.

It was unfortunate that there was another would-be buyer in the room. The powerful pasha of Vidin had sent his representative to the auction and was determined to buy Florenz, even if it meant paying an inflated price.

The bidding increased in increments, with both would-be buyers determined to gain their prize. But the pasha of Vidin had a limitless budget, whereas Baker's was extremely modest. When the bidding reached seventy thousand *kurus* – some eight hundred pounds – he had no option but to withdraw from the sale.

Angered by his failure, Baker took a personal vow to leave Vidin with Florenz in tow, even if it meant resorting to bribery. He secretly approached Ali, the black eunuch who controlled the Finjanjian harem, and struck a deal. In return for a large wad of notes, which he stuffed into Ali's hands, he was allowed to smuggle Florenz out of the compound and into his custody.

It all happened in seconds. Florenz was bundled out of an arched window at the rear of the Finjanjian mansion and helped into Samuel's waiting carriage. Bewildered by what had happened – but happy to have escaped the pasha's clutches – she now made the acquaintance of the English stranger who had tried to buy her.

She spoke at length about her turbulent childhood, unaware

that she was about to embark on further adventures. For she was destined to become one of the great Victorian explorers of central Africa, accompanying Baker on his most arduous voyages into the tropical unknown. She proved an invaluable companion since she spoke fluent Arabic (which she had learned in the harem) as well as Hungarian and German.

The two of them made a deeply unconventional couple. Unmarried until 1865, they headed first to Cairo and together explored the Sudan and Abyssinia. Later from Khartoum, they embarked on a dangerous voyage up the Nile.

At one point they encountered the explorer John Hanning Speke who was returning from Lake Victoria, which he had correctly identified as the source of the Nile.

In conditions of terrible hardship, Samuel and Florence (her name was by now anglicized) pressed on into uncharted territory, exploring the lake regions of Africa and discovering and naming the Murchison Falls and Lake Albert.

After a brief stint in England – where they finally married – they were off again, this time to equatorial Africa. Together they led a bloody military expedition against slave traders, a fight that must have given Florence considerable personal satisfaction. It ended in a victorious battle in Masindi, in today's Uganda.

The Bakers finally returned to England in 1874 and bought an estate in the West Country. Samuel died in 1893, a much feted explorer. Florence outlived her husband by twenty-three years but never received the recognition she deserved for her extraordinary journeys across the Dark Continent. Nor was she presented at court, as might have been expected for someone who had achieved so much.

Queen Victoria adamantly denied her a royal audience on the

grounds that her husband had been 'intimate with his wife before marriage'.

Florence finally died in 1916, by which time the world of her childhood had changed beyond all recognition. The age of harems and eunuchs was in its last twilight, and even the Ottoman Empire, in which she had been sold into slavery, was on the point of permanent collapse.

PART IV

Mein Führer

To sum it all up, I must say that I regret nothing.

ADOLF EICHMANN, 1960

10

Hitler's Final Hours

For the occupants of Hitler's private bunker, the news could scarcely have been bleaker. The Soviet army was advancing so rapidly that it was now within a few hundred yards of the bunker's perimeter fence.

The nearby Schlesischer railway station had already been captured. The Tiergarten was also in Soviet hands and the tunnel in the Voss Strasse was in the process of being occupied. Soon the bunker itself would also be overrun and the Führer would be taken prisoner. Hitler knew all too well that the Third Reich was in its final death throes.

In the small hours of 28–29 April 1945, he summoned a loyal official named Walter Wagner into his private conference room. Wagner's position as city administrator gave him the right to officiate at a wedding ceremony. Hitler announced that he and his long-term mistress, Eva Braun, were to be married without further ado.

The formalities were kept brief for there was no time to lose. The couple declared themselves to be of pure Aryan descent and free from hereditary disease. Then, having given their assent by simple word of mouth, they were declared to be man and wife.

The newlyweds walked out into the corridor to be congratulated by Hitler's faithful secretaries, Gerda Christian and Traudl Junge. They then sat together for several hours, drinking champagne and talking of happier times. The conversation took a rather more depressing turn as Hitler spoke of his impending suicide. National Socialism, he said, was dead. It would never be revived.

His resolve to kill himself was given fresh impetus by the shocking news that he received early in the morning of 29 April. He was told that Mussolini and his mistress, Clara Petacci, had been executed by partisans and strung up by their feet in the Piazzale Loreto in Milan.

'I will not fall into the hands of an enemy who requires a new spectacle to divert his hysterical masses!' he shouted.

In the afternoon of that same day, he had his favourite Alsatian dog Blondi destroyed with poison. His two other dogs were shot by their keeper. Hitler then distributed cyanide capsules to his secretaries for use in extremity. He expressed his regret at not giving them a better parting gift, adding that he wished his generals fighting against Stalin had been as faithful and reliable as they were.

At 2.30 a.m., some twenty faithful servants assembled to greet Hitler as he emerged from his private quarters. He offered them his final farewells and then returned to his private quarters. Everyone was sure that his suicide was imminent.

Yet he was still alive as dawn broke the sky on the following morning and he continued to receive military reports on the situation across Berlin. At 2 p.m., he even sat down to eat lunch with his two secretaries. His SS adjutant, Sturmbannführer Günsche, was meanwhile fulfilling the Führer's orders to acquire 200 litres of petrol.

When Hitler had finished eating, he emerged from his private quarters accompanied by his new wife. Another farewell ceremony took place, this time with Martin Bormann, Joseph Goebbels and others. Eva embraced Traudl Junge and said: 'Take my fur coat as a memory. I always like well-dressed women.'

Hitler then turned to address the little group for a final time. 'It is finished,' he said. 'Goodbye.'

He led Eva back into his private room. Soon afterwards, a single shot was heard.

The group who had gathered to say their farewells to Hitler lingered for a few minutes in the corridor before entering his private room. Hitler himself was lying on the sofa, drenched in blood. He had shot himself through the mouth.

Eva Braun was also sprawled on the sofa. A revolver was by her side but she had not used it. She had swallowed poison instead.

Two SS men were summoned to the room, among them Hitler's faithful servant, Heinz Linge. The two of them wrapped the Führer's body in a blanket and carried it into the courtyard outside.

Eva Braun's body, too, was taken outside. One of the men who helped to carry her body noted she was wearing a blue summer dress made of real silk and that her hair was artificially blonde.

The two corpses were doused in petrol and then set alight. A small group of mourners stood to attention, gave the Nazi salute and then withdrew back inside the bunker. Just beyond the bunker walls, the deep boom of the Soviet artillery lent a theatrical eeriness to the scene.

More petrol had to be poured on the corpses because they would not burn properly. Even after many hours, when most of the flesh had burned away, Hitler's blackened shinbones were still visible.

Shortly before midnight, as the Soviet troops neared the perimeter of the bunker, the two charred corpses were tipped into a bomb crater and covered with soil.

According to Russian reports, the bodies were later exhumed by the Soviet troops who captured the bunker. They were then transferred to Magdeburg in East Germany. It was in Magdeburg – it is claimed – that Hitler's body was finally destroyed by KGB officers in spring 1970.

Yet even that was not quite the end of the story. Two fragments of bone, his jawbone and skull, were preserved as grisly relics. They were last displayed in an exhibition at the Russian Federal Archives in Moscow in April 2000.

11

Seizing Eichmann

He was walking down the street clutching a large bouquet of flowers, a smiling family man by the name of Ricardo Klement. He was looking forward to celebrating his silver wedding anniversary that evening.

When he reached his house on Garibaldi Street in Buenos Aires, the front door was opened by his wife, Vera. Ricardo pushed the flowers into her hands and gave her a kiss. From inside came the sound of happy laughter: the children were already dressed in their party clothes.

Ricardo Klement had no idea that he was being tracked by Mossad secret agents. Nor did he know that those Israeli agents had been on his trail for more than a year.

They were convinced that Klement was not his real name. They had received a tip-off that he was actually Adolf Eichmann, the most senior Nazi still on the run. As Hitler's right-hand man, Eichmann had been responsible for organising the mass deportation of millions of Jews to death camps such as Auschwitz and Treblinka. When the war came to an end, and the Third

Reich collapsed, he had escaped capture by vanishing into thin air. For almost fifteen years he had evaded Mossad.

But in 1959, a German prosecutor named Fritz Bauer received a sensational tip-off. The daughter of one of his Argentina-based friends had been dating a lad named Eichmann (unlike his father, he had retained the old family name). Ignorant of the fact that the girl was Jewish, the young Eichmann bragged of his father's role in exterminating millions of Jews.

Fritz Bauer contacted Mossad, who immediately set to work on the operation to capture Eichmann. Absolute secrecy was paramount: if Eichmann got any hint of Mossad being on his trail, he would disappear again.

The undercover operation was led by Isser Harel, the brilliant head of Mossad. He was determined to bring Eichmann to justice. 'At all the Nuremberg trials of Nazi war criminals this man was pointed to as the head butcher,' he wrote. 'His were the hands that pulled the strings controlling manhunt and massacre.'

As Mossad began to research Eichmann's past, it transpired that he had remained incognito in Europe until 1950, when he was helped to escape to Argentina. He and his family moved several times before settling in Buenos Aires, where he was said to have changed his name to Ricardo Klement.

But Mossad's agents needed to be absolutely certain they were tracking the right man. It was the silver wedding anniversary flowers that provided them with the clinching evidence. They knew that Eichmann's twenty-fifth wedding anniversary was on 21 March 1960. When they saw 'Ricardo Klement' hand the flowers to his wife on the evening of that day, they had confirmation that Klement and Eichmann were one and the same person.

The Mossad operation to capture Eichmann coincided with

Argentina celebrating 150 years of independence. This provided Isser Harel with the perfect cover to smuggle thirty special agents into the country.

Nothing was left to chance. Mossad set up a bogus travel agency in Europe to ensure that there would be no problems with visas or plane connections.

Harel was acutely aware that Mossad was violating Argentinian sovereignty by kidnapping Eichmann: secrecy was therefore of the utmost importance. By 11 May, the Mossad team was ready to swoop.

Harel knew that Eichmann usually returned home from work at around 7.40 p.m. He stationed his agents in the street shortly before this time. Two of them pretended to be repairing the engine of their car. A second Mossad vehicle was parked thirty yards behind the first one.

Two buses arrived but Eichmann was not on them. Harel was about to call off the operation when a third bus pulled up and a middle-aged man alighted. It was Eichmann.

As he neared the Mossad car, one of the Israeli operatives called 'just a moment' before jumping on him. Eichmann was terrified. 'He let out a terrible yell, like a wild beast caught in a trap.'

The other agents bundled Eichmann into the car and drove off at high speed. Eichmann was gagged and his hands and feet were tied together. He was told that he would be shot if he made a sound.

He was taken to a safe house where he was interrogated. He offered no resistance: indeed, he went out of his way to be helpful.

'Gone was the SS officer who once had hundreds of men to carry out his commands,' recalled Harel. 'Now he was frightened and nervous, at times pathetically eager to help.'

Eichmann was held for a week before he could be flown to Israel aboard an El Al flight. The Mossad agents pretended to be helping a brain-damaged patient return to Israel. They faked papers to this effect. To make the ruse more convincing, they drugged Eichmann and carried him onto the waiting plane.

Exactly eleven months after his capture, Eichmann was put on trial in Israel. He was indicted on fifteen criminal charges, including crimes against humanity, war crimes and crimes against the Jewish people. Eichmann's only defence was that he was following orders.

It was not enough to save him. He was convicted on all counts and sentenced to death. He was hanged on the last day of May 1962, in an Israeli prison.

12

The Celebrity Executioner

I t was Friday the 13th and there were thirteen prisoners, all of them awaiting execution: ten men and three women who had sent tens of thousands of concentration camp victims to their deaths. Now, it was their turn to die.

There was never any doubt as to who would undertake the executions. Albert Pierrepoint was Britain's most experienced hangman. He had first been given the job of executioner in 1932, following in the footsteps of his father and uncle. He proved so reliable and efficient that he was promoted to Chief Executioner in 1941. He turned his trade into an art, becoming an expert at double executions, hanging two men at the same time. Now, in December 1945, his services were required to carry out the numerous executions that followed the Nazi war crime trials. The most sensational of these was the hanging of the so-called 'Beasts of Belsen'.

The 'beasts' included Irma Grese, a twenty-one-year-old blonde dairy maid who had joined the SS and got herself transferred to Belsen, where she earned infamy for lashing her Jewish prisoners to death with her riding whip as they were on their way to the gas chambers.

Also convicted was Juana Bormann, who had treated her prisoners with horrific violence, setting her Alsatian dog onto the weak and sick. 'First she egged the dog on and it pulled at the woman [victim's] clothes,' said one witness at her trial. 'Then she was not satisfied with that and made the dog go for her throat.' She, like Irma Grese, was found guilty and sentenced to hang.

The Belsen executions were to be rather different from Pierrepoint's previous hangings. He usually worked with an assistant, but on this occasion he was put in charge of the entire process. It was a job that required meticulous planning. 'I had to supervise the weighings and measuring of the condemned thirteen in order to work out my drops.'

When he first arrived at Bückeburg prison, where the criminals were being held, he was appalled to see that thirteen graves were already being dug for the condemned prisoners. He felt this was unseemly. 'I complained about it to a prison official but was told that nothing could be done to stop it.'

His next duty was to meet the men and women he was due to hang. 'I walked down the corridor and the thirteen Belsen faces were pressed close to the bars.' He was taken aback. 'Never in my experience have I seen a more pitiable crowd of condemned prisoners.'

Pierrepoint had executed scores of people over the previous decade but he had never hanged thirteen in one day and nor had he hanged anyone quite so evil as these prisoners. He expressed a particular interest in meeting Irma Grese.

'She walked out of her cell and came towards us laughing,' he wrote. 'She seemed as bonny a girl as one could ever wish to meet.'

When he asked her age, she paused and gave a weak smile.

Pierrepoint also found himself smiling, 'as if we realised the conventional embarrassment of a woman revealing her age'.

The first of the criminals to be weighed and measured was Josef Kramer, who had killed thousands of victims. He was extremely sullen and answered Pierrepoint's questions with gruff reticence.

The next prisoner, Dr Fritz Klein, had killed 300 victims at a time: he had also killed individual inmates using hypodermic syringes. Pierrepoint found him full of energy and not a bit contrite. '[He] came walking briskly down the corridor and efficiently complied with the formalities.'

Once all the prisoners had been weighed, Pierrepoint had to work out the length of rope that would be needed to kill them. If the drop was too long, it would tear their heads off. If it was too short, it might not break their necks.

Pierrepoint arose at 6 a.m. on Friday 13 December 1945, the day of the executions. He decided to hang the women first, beginning with Irma Grese. She proved a model of calmness, walking slowly to the trap and standing on the white chalk mark.

'As I placed the white cap over her head, she said in her languid voice: "Schnell."' The trapdoor crashed from under her feet and her body twisted as the rope broke her neck. Pierrepoint's first prisoner was dead.

He hanged the two other women before pausing for a muchneeded cup of tea. Then he set to work on the men, adjusting the scaffold so that he could kill them in pairs.

First to go were Josef Kramer and Fritz Klein. They were bound together and then roped by their necks. 'I adjusted the ropes and flew to the lever,' recalled Pierrepoint. Twenty-five seconds later, both were dead.

And so it continued. It was dark by the time all the prisoners had been despatched. Pierrepoint was exhausted and in need of more conventional entertainment: he thoroughly enjoyed himself at the mess party that night.

He was proud to have hanged the 'Beasts of Belsen': it had all gone like clockwork. He would subsequently be called to execute a further 190 Nazi war criminals, including Bruno Tesch, inventor of the gas Zyklon B.

Pierrepoint was a model of efficiency and liked to boast that he could get his clients from their cells to the gallows – and hang them – in under a minute.

He was eventually retired due to failing eyesight at the age of seventy-two. Home Office officials cancelled his contract when they learned that he almost sent his assistant through the trap-door by mistake.

PART V

Get Me Out of Here!

I saw that a boiling red river was coming from another part of the hill and cutting off the escape of the people who were running from their houses. The whole side of the mountain seemed to open and boil down on the screaming people.

ACCOUNT OF HAVIVRA DA IFRILE, ONE OF THREE KNOWN
SURVIVORS OF THE 1906 ERUPTION OF MOUNT PELÉE

13

Trapped on an Iceberg

Wilfred Grenfell had been in many dangerous situations, but none had been quite as precarious as his current one. He was adrift on a floating island of ice and being swept out towards the wild Atlantic Ocean.

The snow-covered coastline of Newfoundland lay far behind him; indeed it had faded to a distant smudge. Ahead lay only danger and death. Grenfell could already hear the sickening slush of sea-ice being ground to pulp by the waves. He knew it was only a matter of time before his own little island of ice would give way beneath him.

Grenfell had taken a huge risk in attempting to cross the ice-bound Newfoundland bay, but he was on a mission of the utmost urgency. He was required at the local hospital, where a young lad lay seriously ill with poisonous gangrene in his leg. The leg needed to be treated – and possibly amputated – if he was to have any chance of survival. In the wilds of rural Newfoundland, Grenfell alone could perform the operation.

The safest and most reliable route to the hospital was along the rough coast path. But it was arduous in winter, for it traversed rocky inlets and snow-bound ravines. Far quicker, though considerably more dangerous, was to cross the sea ice.

Grenfell's journey began well enough. He had the right equipment for crossing the ice, with a change of clothes, snowshoes, rifle and oilskins. He also had a team of six dogs who were to pull his *komatic* or heavy sledge.

But as he pushed out into the frozen bay he suddenly grew alarmed. The heavy swell was breaking the ice into blocks that were held together by wafer-thin skins. Some of these skins had melted, turning the blocks into floating islands known locally as ice-pans.

With considerable effort Grenfell managed to make it across to a stable island of ice. From here, it was a further four miles across slushy ice to the rocky headland. He set off undaunted and was close to the landing point when disaster struck. He suddenly found himself crossing 'sish' – a slush-like porridge of ice. The ice-pans had completely disappeared.

One moment he was afloat; the next, he was sinking. 'There was not a moment to lose. I tore off my oilskins, threw myself on my hands and shouted to my team to go ahead for the shore.'

But the dogs were as frightened as he was and they also began to sink in the slush, along with the sledge. Soon they were flailing in icy water 'like flies in treacle'.

After swimming through the icy water, Grenfell managed to reach a lone ice-pan. With considerable difficulty, he pulled himself onto the ice and then managed to save his dogs as well. But the wind was now whipping off the land and dragging Grenfell's ice-pan relentlessly out to sea.

He was bitterly cold and had lost all his equipment. 'I stood with next to nothing on, the wind going through me and every stitch soaked in ice water.' His only reassurance was the fact that he would meet with a mercifully quick death, for the sea temperature was close to freezing and the waves were mounting in height.

'Immense pans of Arctic ice, surging to and fro on the heavy rolling seas, were thundering into the cliffs like medieval battering rams.'

Grenfell was a born survivor and now used every technique he had been taught. He cut off his moccasins and split them open in order to make a makeshift jacket.

Still freezing, he realized that his only course was to start killing the dogs. He made a slipknot from leather, pulled it over the neck of one of the animals to stop it from biting him and then stabbed it through the heart. He proceeded to hack off the skin and wrap the bloody pelt over his shoulders. He then killed two more dogs and used their skins to keep warm.

By now it was growing dark: he realized that he must have been adrift for many hours. He hadn't eaten for the entire day but managed to keep his hunger at bay by chewing a band of rubber.

Sheer willpower kept him alive through the icy night, with the wind whipping across the ice and causing frostbite in his feet. When the sun finally rose, he tied together the thigh-bones of his slaughtered dogs and slipped his shirt over the end, making a rudimentary flag. It was his last hope of being sighted.

He was by now in a sorry state: 'my poor, gruesome pan was bobbing up and down, stained with blood and littered with carcasses and debris'.

He was unaware that he had been sighted shortly after dawn. A man on the cliffs had seen him drifting out to sea and raised the alarm. Now, rescue was on its way. Four men were rowing with tremendous effort through the slush, aware that their village comrade could not keep himself alive for much longer.

Grenfell didn't see them coming, for he was by now badly afflicted with snow blindness. The first thing he knew about his rescue was the cries of the men's voices.

'As the man in the bow leaped from the boat onto my ice raft and grasped both my hands in his, not a word was uttered.' Grenfell knew that he'd had a very lucky escape. 'We all love life,' he wrote in the account of his adventure. 'I was glad to be back once more with a new lease of it before me.'

Grenfell was also able to bring a new lease of life to the sickly boy who was awaiting him. He went straight to the hospital and successfully operated on his gangrenous leg. The boy went on to make a full recovery.

14

Volcano of Death

It was as if someone had switched off the sun. At exactly 8.02 a.m. on 8 May 1902, the Caribbean town of Saint-Pierre was rocked by a cataclysmic explosion. The sky above Martinique was plunged into instant darkness and the volcano Mount Pelée could be heard to roar like a beast.

When the sky lightened for a moment, the inhabitants turned their gaze to the volcano. They were horrified by what they saw. A vast wall of molten rock was roaring towards them, gathering momentum as it cascaded down the steep slopes above the town. In its wake was an avalanche of superheated gas and dust. The temperature of the flow was in excess of 1,000°C and was vaporizing everything in its path.

Among the 30,000 terrified inhabitants was Léon Compère-Léandre, a local shoemaker. He had been outside when the volcano spectacularly erupted. 'I felt a terrible wind blowing, the earth began to tremble, and the sky suddenly became dark,' he later wrote. 'I turned to go into the house, with great difficulty climbed the three or four steps that separated me from my room, and felt my arms and legs burning, also my body.'

As he collapsed in agony, four other people burst into the room, 'crying and writhing with pain'. It was clear that they had suffered massive internal injuries from the noxious volcanic gases filling the air, even before the main avalanche arrived.

One of the victims was the young daughter of the Delavaud family, whose father had already sought refuge in Léon's house. She was in a terrible state and died almost immediately. The others struggled to their feet, coughing violently as they fled back outside in the hope of finding some avenue of escape.

Léon went into another room, 'where I found the father Delavaud, still clothed and lying on the bed, dead. He was purple and inflated, but the clothing was intact.'

By now Léon was desperate, 'crazed and almost overcome'. Unable to move, he lay on a bed, 'inert and awaiting death'.

The people still outside in the streets were doomed, for there was no hope of outrunning the advancing avalanche. But there were to be a few witnesses to the ensuing disaster – people on boats at the time of the eruption. They watched in appalled fascination as the torrent of toxic rock slammed into the outskirts of the town, flattening everything in its path.

Seconds later, it engulfed the centre of Saint-Pierre. 'The town vanished before our eyes,' said one.

Virtually everyone in Saint-Pierre was killed in seconds, either gassed by the noxious fumes or incinerated by the solid wall of heat. But there were to be a couple of miracle survivors on that bleak morning in 1902.

One hour after the avalanche had struck the town, Léon Compère-Léandre suddenly awoke. He had lost consciousness at the moment the debris reached Saint-Pierre and was in a daze as to what had happened.

He picked his way out of his shattered house and found a scene of absolute desolation. The town of his childhood was a charred and smoking ruin with scarcely a single building left standing. He stumbled over the hot cinders, walking for miles until he eventually left the zone of destruction and reached a village where he told astonished locals the story of his survival.

How he managed to escape the burning avalanche remains a complete mystery. The cloud of toxic gas, boiling dust and molten rock had left him completely unscathed.

But Léon was not the only survivor of that terrible spring day in 1902. One other man emerged alive from the inferno and he was able to recount exactly how he had cheated death on that grim morning.

Louis-Auguste Cyparis had been incarcerated in the city's prison on the day before the eruption, having been involved in a violent pub brawl. He was locked into an underground cell with windowless stone-built walls. The only ventilation came from a grating in the metal door that faced away from the volcano.

Cyparis heard the violent explosion and immediately realised that Mount Pelée had erupted. The sunlight that he could glimpse through the grating vanished in an instant.

Seconds later, scorching air and burning ash began filtering into his cell, causing him severe burns. He urinated on his clothes and stuffed them into the ventilation hole in order to protect himself. He knew that if the ash kept falling, he would soon be trapped in an underground tomb.

A rescue operation began within hours of the eruption. The warship *Suchet* reached the burning town at 12.30 p.m. But the wreckage of Saint-Pierre was still pumping out such ferocious heat that the vessel could not dock until 3 p.m., when the captain finally managed to get ashore.

He was staggered by what he found. Not a building, nor even a tree, was left standing. Everything was charred beyond recognition. The entire 30,000 population was dead.

Except for one. Cyparis was still trapped in his lonely tomb and he would remain there for fully four days until a team of rescuers heard his forlorn cries. He was dug from the compacted ash and helped to safety by his astonished rescuers. He eventually recovered from his burns, was pardoned for his crime and would earn a celebrity of sorts as a performer with Barnum and Bailey's circus.

The only other survivor of that terrible morning was a young girl named Haviva Da Ifrile. Her escape was even more bizarre than the other two. She was found adrift in a boat, unconscious but alive. She had no recollection of how she got there.

15

The Female Robinson Crusoe

In the third week of August, 1923, the good ship *Donaldson* arrived at the desolate shores of Wrangel Island, far to the north of Siberia. The crew were bringing supplies to five colonists left here two years earlier and were expecting to find them all in good health. Instead, they found just one of those colonists, a half-starved young woman named Ada Blackjack. She was gaunt and sick, but alive. And she had an incredible story to tell.

Two years earlier, Ada Blackjack had volunteered to take part in one of the strangest missions in the history of colonization. She and four others were to test the feasibility of living on ice-bound Wrangel Island.

The 1921 colonial experiment was the brainchild of Arctic explorer Vilhjalmur Stefansson. One of his key goals was to claim the land for Canada. Another was to prove that this bleak land was habitable. Stefansson entertained hopes of establishing an extreme tourism company that would offer adventure tours of this remote outpost.

Four of Stefansson's team were men: three Americans named Lorne Knight, Milton Galle and Fred Maurer, and a Canadian called Allan Crawford. They had impressive academic credentials but rather less experience of surviving in extreme Arctic conditions.

The fifth colonist was a young Inuit woman named Ada Blackjack. Ada's husband had died some years earlier leaving her destitute. She also had a child with chronic tuberculosis, an illness that required costly treatment. She decided to join the expedition for a year, lured by the promise of a good salary. She was officially employed as the team's seamstress.

Just twenty-five years of age, Ada was an odd choice to accompany the mission. She knew nothing about hunting or trapping and had never before lived off the land. She didn't even know how to build an igloo.

The rest of the team expressed deep misgivings when they learned that she had been selected to join them. They said she would be a hindrance to the others and was too frail to survive the harsh conditions. But their concerns were overruled by Vilhjalmur Stefansson. Ada Blackjack was officially employed as the fifth member of the team.

On 16 September 1921, the five colonists were left on barren Wrangel Island, far to the north of Siberia. Stefansson, who declined to accompany the expedition, believed the island to be so well stocked with wildlife that he left the colonists with enough food for just six months. He promised to send a supply ship in the following summer: in the meantime, the five would have to fend for themselves.

The mission got off to a flying start. The colonists built a large snow house and had great success in hunting the local wildlife. They managed to kill ten polar bears, thirty seals and many geese and duck. They were confident that they could survive until the ship's return.

But the promised vessel failed to materialize and the five settlers realized they faced a long and arduous autumn. They soon ran short of tea, coffee and sugar. They then ate the last of their flour and beans. As the November gale whipped in a ferocious Arctic winter, the wild game disappeared and the five found themselves critically short of food. Worse still, Lorne Knight developed a serious illness.

On 28 January 1923, Crawford, Galle and Maurer decided to attempt to traverse the frozen Chukchi Sea in order to reach the Siberian mainland. They wanted to alert people to the fact they were in desperate need of help.

The three of them were never seen again and their fate remains a mystery. Either they fell through the ice and drowned in the freezing seawater or they froze to death in an Arctic blizzard.

Lorne Knight had meanwhile taken a turn for the worse. He was now suffering from acute scurvy and could scarcely move his joints. He was nursed by Ada until April, when his body gave up the ghost. Ada now found herself utterly alone in this icebound wilderness.

She had no idea how to hunt and had never even fired the rifle that had been left behind. But she soon worked out how to use it and managed to kill seals, foxes and ducks. She then stewed the meat to make it more palatable.

She managed to prevent the fire from going out, even though fuel was scarce, and kept insanity at bay by reading the Bible. But as another summer slipped into autumn, she grew increasingly weak. She knew that her own death was now inevitable.

She had given up hope of ever being rescued when she sighted a vessel on the horizon. It was the *Donaldson*, which arrived at Wrangel Island on 23 August. The crew were astonished to stumble across Ada Blackjack and even more surprised to learn that three of her male comrades were missing and the fourth was dead.

When her story reached the outside world, the newspapers labelled her the 'female Robinson Crusoe'. Her survival, they said, was nothing short of a miracle. She had received no training in survival techniques, yet had kept herself alive for twenty-three months.

Ada did not take kindly to the media circus and shunned the publicity. She wanted nothing more than to be reunited with her son, using the expedition salary to take him to Seattle in order to cure his tuberculosis.

But the fact that she had a sickly child – who was eventually cured – brought a new dimension to the story. Ada became an unwitting celebrity, heralded as a heroic survivor in books and magazines. 'Her physical stomach wasn't a bit more adapted to seal oil and blubber than theirs [the men's],' wrote one. 'But in Ada's heart there was a fire that isn't easily blown out.'

Ada never went back to Wrangel Island, but she did return to the Arctic and eventually made it her home. The freezing climate seems to have suited her, for she finally died at the ripe old age of eighty-five.

PART VI

O What a Lovely War!

ashdladiin dóó ba'ąą náhást'éidi mííl tsosts'idi

neeznádiin dízdįįhastaa

THE NUMBER 59,746 IN NAVAJO, THE HIGHLY COMPLEX
NATIVE AMERICAN LANGUAGE USED FOR AMERICAN
BATTLEFIELD COMMUNICATIONS DURING THE
SECOND WORLD WAR

16

The Last Post

American conscript Henry Gunther was appalled when he arrived at the battlefields of northern France in the winter of 1917. The mud-filled trenches were bleaker than he was expecting and the atmosphere of decay hung heavy in the air.

Gunther had been drafted into the 313th Regiment, known as Baltimore's Own, just a few weeks earlier. He was a supply sergeant, responsible for the clothing of his regiment.

Now, staring across a landscape of shattered buildings and trees, he felt profoundly depressed. He had no desire to fight in a war that was thousands of miles from his native land. It was a world away from the book-keeping job he had at the Bank of Baltimore. Homesick and depressed, he wrote to a friend complaining of the 'miserable conditions' in which he found himself. He told that friend to do whatever he could to dodge the draft.

It was unfortunate for Gunther that his letter was read by an army censor. The censor was appalled by such defeatist sentiments and reported Gunther to his superior. There was never any doubt that he would be punished for his lack of patriotism, but the chosen punishment was to leave him with a deep psychological scar. He was demoted from sergeant to private, bringing shame on both himself and his family.

'He brooded a great deal over his reduction in rank and became obsessed with a determination to make good before his officers and fellow soldiers.' So wrote James M. Cain, a war reporter for the *Baltimore Sun*. 'He was worried because he thought himself suspected of being a German sympathizer. The regiment went into action a few days after he was reduced [in rank] and from the start he displayed the most unusual willingness to expose himself to all sorts of risks.'

The question uppermost in Gunther's mind was how he could best 'make good' for his perceived lack of patriotism. The war was rapidly drawing to a close and there were already rumours that the German army was on the point of surrendering. As dawn broke on 11 November, Gunther knew that he needed to do something in the very near future.

In common with most soldiers on that chilly morning, Gunther had no idea that the armistice had already been signed. At 5.20 a.m., British, French and German officials had met in a railway carriage to the north of Paris and brought the First World War to an end. Now, all they needed to do was transmit the news to the troops on the ground.

This was not easy. Many battalions were using old and inadequate communications and many more were completely cut off from their command centres. The generals realized that it would take time to notify all the troops. They decreed that the peace would not come into effect until 11 a.m.

Henry Gunther and his men learned of the approaching armistice at 10.30 a.m. Their wisest course of action would have been to lie low for the next half an hour until it was officially declared. Instead, they continued their march towards Chaumont-devant-Damvillers, a village near Metz, arriving at the outskirts as it approached eleven o'clock.

As they made their way along the country road, they found their path blocked by two enemy machine-gun posts. The Germans were under orders to open fire, but they deliberately shot into the air so as not to claim any more lives.

Gunther's comrades were touched by the action of the Germans, who were clearly aware of the impending armistice. But Gunther himself saw things rather differently. Aware that he had just a couple of minutes to make a heroic impact, he expressed his outrage at the fact that they had fired their guns. Against the orders of his sergeant (and close friend) Ernest Powell, he made a dramatic charge through the thick fog towards the German machine guns.

According to reporter James M. Cain, 'he was fired by a desire to demonstrate, even at the last minute, that he was courageous and all-American'.

The German soldiers were horrified when they saw their position being charged by a lone soldier. 'They waved at him and called out, in such broken English as they could, to go back, that the war was over. He paid no heed to them, however, and kept on firing a shot or two as he went.'

When the Germans saw that he was determined to keep up his forlorn charge, they had no option but to turn their machine gun on him. Gunther fell in action at 10.59 a.m. and is officially recognized as the last soldier to be killed in the First World War.

'Almost as he fell', noted his divisional record, 'the gunfire died away and an appalling silence prevailed.'

The army would eventually restore him to the rank of sergeant and also award him two posthumous medals for gallantry. Henry Gunther emerged from the war as both its last victim and its final hero.

17

To Hell and Back

Audie Murphy was short, skinny and underage, hardly suitable material for a fighting soldier in the Second World War. The American army certainly thought him inadequate when he tried to enroll for service in December 1941. They rejected him not only on the grounds of his youth – he was just sixteen-and-a-half – but also because of his slight frame.

Murphy made a second attempt to enlist in the following year. He was once again rejected, not only by the regular army but also by the Marine Corp, the Airborne and the navy.

After much persistence, he finally succeeded in getting himself enrolled in the army and was sent for training in Texas. He proved unsuitable in every respect, vindicating the army's previous decisions to reject him. During one training session he fainted from exhaustion. His company commander was so alarmed that he tried to move him to an army cookery school.

But Murphy was determined to prove the doubters wrong and he was to do so in style. The first inkling of his bravery came in September 1943, when his scouting party was ambushed by

German machine guns on the Italian front. Murphy returned fire and killed all five Germans. His unexpected heroism earned him promotion to sergeant.

He fought in further battles in Italy and France and began to display a reckless determination to win at all costs. He was at his most efficient leading small groups of men into attack against an overwhelmingly superior enemy.

After participating in Operation Dragoon in Southern France, he and his men were transferred to Alsace, where fighting between the Allies and crack German soldiers was at its most intense.

His platoon came under heavy fire while crossing a vineyard. Murphy managed single-handedly to seize one of the enemy machine guns and then turned it on the Germans, killing or wounding them. His action was extraordinarily brave and won him the Distinguished Service Cross.

Shortly afterwards, his best friend was killed by a group of Germans who were pretending to surrender. Murphy was so disgusted by their underhand trick that he charged them, killing six, wounding two and taking eleven of them prisoner.

During seven weeks of tough fighting, Murphy's division suffered 4,500 casualties. Murphy himself was always in the thick of it. He received two silver stars for heroic action, was promoted to second lieutenant and elevated to platoon leader. Although he had proved himself one of the bravest soldiers fighting in Alsace, his moment of glory still lay before him.

In January 1945, he and his men were moved to the woods near Holtzwihr. This territory was strategically vital to the Allied advance and had only recently been captured. It was no less crucial to the Germans, who were determined to recover their ground.

Murphy's unusual leadership skills had by now so impressed his superiors that they made him a company commander. His orders were to block any German advance.

On 26 January, his men went into action against the enemy. It was bitterly cold – minus 10°C – with an arctic wind and two feet of snow on the ground. The men fought with tenacious courage but a ferocious firefight steadily reduced them to an effective fighting force of just 19 men out of their original 128.

Murphy realized that the remnants of his company couldn't hold out any longer and ordered them to retreat into the forest. But he had no intention of following their retreat. He clambered onto a burned-out tank destroyer and used his lone position to direct American artillery fire coming from the rear.

'I loved that artillery,' he later recalled. 'I could see Kraut soldiers disappear in clouds of smoke and snow, hear them scream and shout, yet they came on and on as though nothing would stop them.'

The Germans slowly advanced, despite the bombing, and were soon within fifty yards of Murphy's hiding place. When battalion headquarters asked him to inform them of the enemy's position, Murphy replied: 'If you just hold the phone a minute, I'll let you talk to one of the bastards.'

He continued to spray the advancing troops with bullets, killing some fifty German soldiers in one sustained burst of fire. At one point he spied a group of soldiers hiding in a nearby ditch. 'I pressed the trigger and slowly traversed the barrel – the bodies slumped in a stack position.'

Murphy only stopped fighting when his line of communication to headquarters was cut by enemy artillery. He was badly injured yet he continued to lead his men for the next two days until the area around Holtzwihr and the Colmar Canal was finally cleared of Germans. It was an exceptional feat of war and all the more remarkable given the fact that he had been twice rejected by the army on the grounds that he was too feeble to fight.

On 2 June 1945, Murphy was presented with the Medal of Honor, America's highest honour. It was the peak of his military career, one that ended with thirty-two additional medals, ribbons, citations and badges.

Murphy would later become a Hollywood star, acting in the film of his own experiences, *To Hell and Back*. But his life was cut tragically short when he died in a plane crash in 1971. He was just forty-six.

When asked what motivated him to fight single-handed against a company of German infantry, he replied: 'They were killing my friends.'

18

Let's Talk Gibberish

Japanese code-breaker Seizo Arisue had every reason to feel satisfied with himself. He and his team had met with great success in cracking the secret transmissions of the American high command. Many of these deciphered intercepts concerned the deployment of troops, giving the Japanese a significant advantage.

But in the spring of 1945, Seizo Arisue found himself completely perplexed by the new code being used by the American army. He spent many hours attempting to decipher it, but all to no avail. *Ahkehdiglini* was one of the words. *Tsahahdzoh* was another. And so it continued for several pages. Arisue could only conclude that it had been written in gibberish.

The messages were indeed indecipherable, just as the Americans intended. They were sending them in Navajo, a highly complex Native American language that very few people in the world were able to speak.

The idea of using the Navajo language for battlefield communications was first suggested by Philip Johnston, the son of an

American missionary. He was one of the few non-Navajos in the world who spoke the language fluently.

Johnston knew that Native American languages had been successfully used for battlefield communications in the First World War. He also knew that Navajo would present the Japanese codebreakers with a formidable challenge. Its tortuous syntax and numerous dialects rendered it unintelligible to anyone who had not been exposed to it for years.

The US army first tried out Johnson's ingenious idea in the spring of 1942. It proved so foolproof that they began drafting more Navajo speakers into the army's ranks. They became known as the code-talkers and they were to play a crucial role in the war in the Far East.

Among them was Samuel Tso, a twenty-three-year-old Navajo speaker who directed communications for the United States Marine Corps during the battle for Iwo Jima. He and his team of six code-talkers transmitted hundreds of strategically vital commands during the month-long battle.

The commands were relayed as a string of seemingly unrelated Navajo words that bore no obvious relation to battlefield terms. This was because words like 'machine gun' and 'battleship' didn't exist in Navajo.

To overcome this problem of vocabulary, Tso's team used designated Navajo words to describe military hardware. 'Whale' was used to describe a battleship, 'iron-fish' to describe a submarine and 'hummingbird' to describe a fighter plane.

But the code was a great deal more sophisticated than that. One of the basic principals was that specific Navajo words were chosen to represent individual letters of the Roman alphabet. To represent the letter 'a', for example, Tso could use any of the following: *wollachee* (ant), *belasana* (apple) or *tsenill* (axe). These words had one key element in common: when translated into English, they all started with the letter 'a'.

Tso and his team sent and received dozens of commands each day. When they received a coded message, their first task was to translate the Navajo words into English. They would then use the first letter of each word to spell out the message. And this is why it proved so impossible for the Japanese to crack. Any code-breaker attempting to read the cipher had to know the meaning of the Navajo word in English. Since there was no Navajo dictionary, they found themselves up against an impossible task.

Tso's team transmitted information on tactics, troop movements and other battlefield communications. They were highly skilled and extremely accurate. As the US Marines fought their way up the heavily defended beaches of Iwo Jima, the code-talkers more than proved their worth.

Major Howard Connor, 5th Marine Division signal officer, was adamant that Tso's men had led the Marines to victory: 'Were it not for the Navajos, the Marines would never have taken Iwo Jima.'

The Japanese code-breakers worked around the clock in their quest to crack the Navajo code, but never succeeded in deciphering a single message.

Philip Johnston's idea of using Navajo had proved to be an inspired one. The use of this indecipherable language had saved tens of thousands of lives.

PART VII

Dial M for Murder

It was kept in a chamber and was a great fowl somewhat bigger than the largest Turkey cock, and so legged and footed, but stouter and thicker and of more erect shape, coloured before like the breast of a young cock pheasant.

SIR HAMON L'ESTRANGE IS SHOWN A LIVE DODO
IN LONDON, 1638. WITHIN TWENTY-FIVE YEARS
THE DODO WAS EXTINCT.

19

Good Ship *Zong*

Captain Luke Collingwood was used to grim voyages across the Atlantic, but this one had been worse than most.

Dysentery, diarrhoea and smallpox had already claimed the lives of seven of the crew aboard the *Zong*. The slave cargo had suffered a far higher mortality rate. More than sixty had died since leaving the shores of Africa.

As Captain Collingwood searched in vain for the coast of Jamaica, he grew increasingly alarmed. He knew that the ship's insurers would not cover the cost of his lost human cargo. Since each slave was worth about £30, he stood to lose a fortune.

On 29 November 1781, he was struck by a macabre idea, one that could turn loss into profit. At a meeting with the *Zong*'s officers, he suggested that they throw the slaves overboard. There was a sinister logic to his reasoning. If his slaves died of illness, their insurance value was lost. But if they were thrown overboard in order to preserve the ship's scant supply of water (and thereby save the lives of others), an insurance claim would be valid under a legal principle known as the 'general average'. It allowed the captain of a ship to sacrifice some of his 'passengers' in order to save others.

The First Mate of the *Zong*, James Kelsall, was appalled by the captain's proposal. He said it was cold-blooded murder. But Collingwood disagreed, insisting that it would be 'less cruel to throw the sick wretches into the sea than to suffer them to linger out a few days, under the disorder with which they were afflicted'.

After much persuasion, Kelsall changed his mind and reluctantly agreed with the captain and other officers. The weakest slaves were to be pitched overboard that very day.

Collingwood went below decks to select his first 'parcel' of victims. He decided to concentrate on the women and children, probably because he knew that they would put up less of a struggle. A total of fifty-four were hurled off the ship and could be seen flailing in the sea before eventually weakening and drowning.

Two days later, on 1 December, Collingwood elected to throw out another 'parcel': this time, his forty-two victims were all men. They drowned so quickly, and with such little effort on the part of the captain and his crew, that Collingwood decided to pitch even more slaves overboard. He was intent on getting the largest possible sum of money from the ship's insurers. He ordered another thirty-six to be thrown into the ocean.

But this third batch of victims were made of stronger stuff and vehemently refused to go to their deaths without a struggle. Collingwood's men were forced to chain them by the ankle and weigh their feet with balls of iron so they would sink immediately.

'The arms of twenty-six were fettered with irons and the savage crew proceeded with the diabolical work, casting them down to join their comrades of the former days.' So reads a contemporary account of the massacre.

Ten of the slaves were so terrified by their fate that they leaped overboard before the captain had the chance to have them chained.

Three weeks after the last murders, the *Zong* finally reached Jamaica with 208 slaves still aboard. They sold for an average price of £36 each, earning Collingwood a substantial profit even before he made his insurance claim. But he did not have long to enjoy his money: he died within three days of making landfall.

His death might have been the end of a sordid and macabre tale, but there was to be an extraordinary postscript, one that caused a sensation in Georgian England.

The ship's owners expressed their full support for what the late Captain Collingwood had done and filed an insurance claim for the 132 slaves that had been thrown overboard. They hoped to recuperate nearly £4,000 in jettisoned 'cargo'.

Thus began a court case that was marked by callousness, cynicism and sheer human greed. The jury were in agreement with the owners and insisted that the insurers pay up the money for the drowned slaves. But the insurers appealed against the decision and asked for the case to be retried. This time, it was to be heard before the Lord Chief Justice, Lord Mansfield.

Those who hoped for a more enlightened approach from Lord Mansfield were quickly disappointed. 'The case of slaves,' he said, 'was the same as if horses had been thrown overboard. The question was, whether there was not an absolute necessity for throwing them over board to save the rest.'

A hitherto unknown fact was now brought before the court. The ship's owners had argued that the slaves were killed because there was not enough water on board. But this was not true.

When the ship arrived at Jamaica, it still had more than 420 imperial gallons of stored water.

This ought to have proved the turning point: Collingwood and his crew were clearly guilty of cold-blooded murder. Yet the new evidence was deemed to be of no consequence and the *Zong*'s owners ultimately won the day. The insurers were forced to pay up for the 'cargo' that had been dumped at sea.

The English abolitionist Granville Sharp was appalled by the verdict and tried to bring forward a case of murder. This was brushed aside by Lord Mansfield.

'What is this claim that human people have been thrown overboard?' he said. 'This is a case of chattels or goods. Blacks are goods and property; it is madness to accuse these well-serving honourable men of murder.'

20

The Suspicions of Inspector Dew

In the early hours of 1 February 1910, the inhabitants of Hilldrop Crescent in North London were shaken from their sleep by a muffled scream. It was followed by a short silence and then an anguished plea for mercy. A few seconds later there was a loud retort that sounded like a gunshot.

The commotion came from number 39, home to Dr Hawley Crippen and his wife, Cora. It was obvious to everyone that something deeply disturbing was taking place inside the house. But no one thought to intervene and on the following morning, when everyone left their houses for work, they chose not to mention the noises in the night.

Dr Crippen greeted his neighbours as usual and found himself warmly greeted in return. He then took himself off to the Music Hall Ladies Guild where his wife, who used the stage name Belle, was honorary treasurer.

He handed the guild a letter, purportedly written by Belle, in which she tendered her resignation. The letter explained how she had to make an urgent voyage to America in order to visit a near relative who was gravely ill.

This news caused surprise but no suspicion. Belle was American, like her husband, and there was no reason to suppose that either of them were telling anything but the truth.

A few weeks after Belle's supposed departure, a new woman moved into Dr Crippen's home. Her name was Miss Ethel Le Neve, a demure and attractive secretary. Aged twenty-seven, she was twenty years younger than him.

Ethel caused quite a stir when she attended the Music Hall Ladies Ball later that month. Not only did she accompany Dr Crippen as his apparent partner, but she was also noticed to be wearing one of Belle's brooches.

Belle's music-hall friends were by now deeply suspicious of what might have happened to their old friend. They went so far as to make enquiries in America as to her possible whereabouts. But it was to no avail. There were no records of Belle having returned to her homeland.

They were now so concerned for her safety they contacted Scotland Yard to inform them of her disappearance. The case was assigned to Chief Inspector Walter Dew, whose first port of call was Dr Crippen's office in New Oxford Street.

Crippen proved a master of composure. He told the inspector that Belle had run off with a lover, a boxer named Brice Miller, and that he'd been too humiliated to admit the truth to his friends.

Inspector Dew swallowed every word. He asked for permission to search the house in Hilldrop Crescent, but only as a formality, and found nothing to awaken his suspicions. As far as he was concerned, the doctor was in the clear.

Crippen was deeply shaken by the enquiries from Scotland

Yard. He was concerned that Inspector Dew would find holes in his story and question him again. This was something he wanted to avoid at all costs.

He took the dramatic decision to flee the country with Ethel in tow. He explained to her that they would be happier, and safer, in America. They would also be away from Scotland Yard.

When Inspector Dew attempted to make contact with the doctor about some minor discrepancies in his account – and learned that he and his secretary had left England – he ordered a more thorough search of the house. This time, events took a more serious turn.

On 13 July, police found a decaying human body in the cellar. It was headless, limbless and in a gruesome state of decomposition. The rotting remains were found to contain traces of hyoscine. Detectives next discovered that Dr Crippen had purchased just such a poison days before his wife's supposed departure.

Two days after the exhumation of the body, Scotland Yard issued a warrant for Dr Crippen's arrest.

But Crippen and Ethel were by now on their way to Canada, having boarded the SS *Montrose* sailing from Antwerp. They registered themselves as father and son – Ethel looked remarkably boyish – and might have deceived everyone on board had it not been for their indiscreet behaviour.

Just hours after setting sail, the ship's captain, Henry Kendall, noticed 'father' and 'son' behaving in an intimate fashion behind the lifeboats. Alarmed by their behaviour – and deeply suspicious – he checked the 'wanted' descriptions in the newspapers. He realized that they answered to the description of Crippen and his lover.

Kendall wired his suspicions to Scotland Yard, whose officers acted immediately. Inspector Dew was able to board the SS

Laurentic, which was on the point of setting sail across the Atlantic, and found himself in a desperate chase to overtake the *Montrose* before it reached Canada.

At around 9 p.m. on the morning of 31 July, in thick St Lawrence fog, the inspector boarded the *Montrose*, purporting to be one of several 'pilots' helping to steer the ship to its berth.

Sighting Dr Crippen, he removed his pilot's hat and shook the doctor by the hand. Crippen froze: he immediately recognized Dew and realized the game was up. 'Thank God it's all over' were his only words as allowed himself to be handcuffed.

Dr Crippen and Ethel Le Neve were immediately charged with 'murder and mutilation' and sent back to England in order to be tried by London's Central Criminal Court.

Crippen protested his innocence, but to no avail. He was found guilty of wilful murder and hanged in prison in November 1910.

Ethel Le Neve was acquitted of any wrongdoing and subsequently fled to America, sailing on the day that Crippen was hanged. And that seemed to be the end of a brutal and tragic story.

But there was to be a surprising postscript, one that has turned the case on its head. Recent mitochondrial DNA evidence suggests that Crippen may have been innocent after all. Working from a sample of blood held at Royal London Hospital Archives, a team of American forensic scientists have compared Belle's DNA with samples taken from one of her surviving relatives.

The results are startling and highlight two key facts: first, the body in the cellar was not Belle. Secondly, it was not even female.

According to Dr David Foran, head of forensic science at Michigan State University, 'that body cannot be Cora [Belle] Crippen, we're certain of that'.

If he is correct, and no one is doubting the results of his tests, then Crippen may be innocent of the crime for which he was hanged.

Two weeks before his execution he wrote: 'I am innocent and some day evidence will be found to prove it.'

The recent DNA analysis may yet clear his name.

21

Dead as a Dodo

They had endured nine long days adrift in a longboat with only their own urine to drink. They were half-crazed by dehydration, hunger and the relentless tropical sun.

But now, as Dutch seadog Volkert Evertszoon and his fellow mariners were washed ashore at a remote islet, they rubbed their eyes in disbelief. The place was home to scores of flightless birds. They waddled along the beach in a most undignified fashion and showed no fear when confronted by the newly arrived men. 'They were larger than geese but not able to fly,' wrote Evertszoon. 'Instead of wings they had small flaps.'

Evertszoon and his comrades could scarcely believe their luck. They had watched their crippled vessel *Arnhem* sink beneath the waves, convinced that they would die a lingering death in their longboat. But here on the Ile d'Ambre, off the east coast of Mauritius, there was enough food to keep them alive for months.

They were to be the last eyewitnesses of the hapless dodo, a bird on the verge of extinction. Indeed, it was almost certainly their empty bellies that led to the dodo's final demise in the spring of 1662.

Ever since the bird had first been sighted in Mauritius in the 1590s, it had been ruthlessly hunted for food. The introduction of pigs had further depleted their number. Indeed the only reason why the bird had survived on Ile d'Ambre – but nowhere else in Mauritius – is that it was the last remaining islet without any pigs.

The dodo did not make for an appetizing feast: it was widely known as the 'loathsome bird' on account of its disgusting taste. But it was extremely easy to catch and the sailors who hunted it were often so hungry that anything was better than the putrid salt-pork they had on board.

One ship's commander declared that dodos were at their most palatable if cooked slowly and over a low heat. 'Their belly and breast are of a pleasant flavour and easily masticated,' wrote Wybrand van Warwijck in 1598.

Such culinary delights were far from the minds of Volkert Evertszoon and his men when they stepped ashore on Ile d'Ambre. Their needs were simple – food – and they were delighted to find that the native dodos were so tame.

'They were not shy at all,' wrote Evertszoon, 'because they very likely were not used to see men pursuing them, and which became us exceedingly well, having neither barrel nor ammunition to shoot them.'

The birds seemed intrigued by the unwashed mariners who had intruded on their realm. 'They stared at us and remained quiet where they stood, not knowing whether they had wings to fly away or legs to run off, and suffering us to approach them as close as we pleased.'

The slaughter began within hours of landing. Evertszoon and

his men drove a flock of the birds into one place 'in such a manner that we could catch them with our hands'. No sooner had they caught one lot than another flock 'came running as fast as they could to its assistance, and by which they were caught and made prisoners also'.

A diet of dodo meat was neither appetizing nor balanced, but it kept the men alive for the three months until they were rescued by the English ship *Truro*.

Evertszoon did not record whether he and his men killed all the dodos on the islet. But it is highly probable that they did, for there were no further sightings in the years that followed. When the Dutch hunter Isaac Lamotius recorded seeing dodos in 1688, he was referring to a different bird. By the time he was writing, the flightless red rail had been given the same Dutch name: *dodaers*.

Unless new evidence comes to light, it seems likely that Evertszoon and his men ate the hapless dodo into extinction.

PART VIII

The Great Escape

*Laden with the weight of human blood and believed
to have banqueted on human flesh*

THE *HOBART TOWN GAZETTE*'S OPINION OF ESCAPED
CONVICT (AND SELF-CONFESSED CANNIBAL)
ALEXANDER PEARCE.

22

A Sting in the Tale

Walter Harris had a nose for a good story and this one seemed better than most. As Morocco correspondent for *The Times*, he knew that violent battles and skirmishes always made good copy.

On a blistering afternoon in June 1903, he was brought news of a bloody onslaught taking place near the town of Zinat. Not wishing to miss out on the action, he climbed onto his horse and headed towards the fighting.

As he approached Zinat, the air was filled with an ominous silence. 'The whole country was absolutely deserted,' he wrote. 'Not a single person, not a head of cattle, was to be seen.'

He was riding across the empty plain when a single volley rang out. Sensing danger, he spurred his horse and rode away from the spot where the gun had been fired.

But as he entered a deep gully, he saw he had fallen into an ambush. 'From every side sprung out tribesmen and in a second or two I was a prisoner, surrounded by thirty or forty men.'

It did not take long for Harris to discover the identity of his captor. It was the dreaded Mulai Ahmed er Raisuli, the most powerful bandit of northern Morocco.

Raisuli ruled his fiefdom with appalling brutality. His favourite punishment was burning out his captives' eyes with heated copper coins. 'By nature he was, and is, cruel,' wrote Harris, 'and the profession he had adopted' – that of bandit – 'gave him unlimited scope to exhibit his cruelty.'

The Englishman's life was in great danger. Raisuli and his bandit tribesmen were convinced that Harris was a supporter of the Moroccan sultan, whose troops had only recently regained much ground in the area.

Raisuli had often argued that capturing Christians was entirely legitimate. He also said that torturing them or even killing them were not crimes, 'because they were commissioned by Allah'.

He led Harris to an underground cell and locked him inside. The room was dark and stank of putrid flesh. It took time for Harris's eyes to get accustomed to the gloom, but when they did he was in for a terrible shock.

'The first object that attracted my eyes was a body lying in the middle of the room. It was the corpse of a man and formed a ghastly spectacle. Stripped of all clothing and shockingly mutilated, the head had been roughly hacked off and the floor all round was swimming in blood.'

Harris had a great deal of experience of life in Morocco and had also written at length about Raisuli. He tried to keep calm and to assess the situation with a clear head. He reckoned that he was worth more to Raisuli alive, as a hostage that could be used as a bargaining chip.

But he became increasingly concerned when he was led from his cell in order to witness an even more gruesome cadaver than the one sharing his cell.

'A ghastly sight,' he later wrote. 'The summer's heat had already caused the corpse to discolour and swell. An apple had been stuck in the man's mouth and both his eyes had been gouged out.'

He was informed that the same treatment awaited him if he tried to play any tricks.

The British Minister, Sir Arthur Nicolson, learned of Harris's capture and tentatively opened negotiations with Raisuli. The bandit had a number of demands, the most important of which was the release of his fifty-six blood relatives. These were being held alongside hundreds of other bandits in the sultan's prisons in Tangier and Larache. The sultan would have executed them long ago, if only he knew which of them were related to Raisuli.

After much wrangling a deal of sorts was struck. Twelve prisoners would be released in exchange for Harris's freedom. But Raisuli proved a slippery captor and kept raising the number, aware that he was holding an extremely valuable Christian captive.

Harris was caught in an impossible predicament. Yet he held a few cards and he was determined to play them with skill. He persuaded Raisuli to tell him the names of all fifty-six relatives that he wanted released. He promised to send this list to Tangier in order that Nicolson could exert his influence to win their freedom. Raisuli did exactly as Harris requested, unaware that he had fallen headlong into a trap.

'You propose to kill me,' said Harris to the bandit chief. 'Possibly you will do so, but you have kindly given me a list of all your relations who are in the Moorish prison. This list is now in Tangier. You will have the satisfaction of killing me, but remember this – on fifty-six consecutive days one of your sons or brothers or nephews will be executed, one each morning.'

Shortly afterwards Harris was released by a furious Raisuli.

The Times correspondent delighted in his trick and took great relish in describing it in his memoirs.

'It was a splendid bluff,' he wrote, 'and I felt the greatest delight in using it.' Not only had he saved his own life, but he had also made a mockery of Raisuli and his tribesmen. 'They swore and cursed and threatened, but to no avail.'

Not for the first time – and nor for the last – Walter Harris had got the upper hand.

23

And Then There Were None

There were eight of them at the outset, convicts making their escape from a penal colony in Van Diemen's Land, today's Tasmania. Their leader was Alexander Pearce, a pockmarked Irishman with a hot head and a reputation for violence. He, in common with his fellow convicts, had been incarcerated in the dreaded Macquarie Harbour penal settlement on Tasmania's remote west coast.

In September 1822, Pearce was working in a labour gang and made his escape by stealing a boat. Seven others jumped into the boat and made their getaway with him.

They were a motley band of thieves, highwaymen and common criminals: Matthew Travers, Alexander Dalton, Robert Greenhill, John Mather, William Kennerly, Thomas Bodenham and Edward 'Little' Brown.

The men rowed unnoticed to the far side of the bay and then sank their stolen boat before making their way into the dense forest. Their goal was the settlement of Hobart at the mouth of the Derwent, where they hoped to steal a ship and sail for England.

They were unaware that to reach Hobart meant traversing some of the most rugged and inhospitable terrain in Australia. The weather only added to their woes. The rain tipped down relentlessly, soaking them to the bone. As the chill wind whipped at their scant clothing, some of them began to complain that they were unable to keep up.

One of the men, William Kennerly, made a cruel but telling jest about their lack of food. 'I am so weak,' he said, 'that I could eat a piece of man.' It soon transpired that he was not joking. He suggested that they should kill the weakest of their company and eat him.

Not everyone agreed. Even though they were hardened criminals, several spoke out against cold-blooded murder. But Robert Greenhill sided with Kennerly. Deranged by hunger, he singled out Alexander Dalton and decided to act immediately, picking up his axe and smashing it into Dalton's skull. He was killed instantly.

Greenhill's comrade-in-arms Matthew Travers willingly joined the bloodletting. 'With a knife [he] also came and cut his throat . . . we tore out his insides and cut off his head.' The remaining seven men divided Dalton into equal portions and ate him.

Even so, the meal proved poor sustenance and did little to help them regain their strength. Two of the men soon fell behind the others and were lost. Both would eventually be recaptured by local guards: both would die soon after.

The remaining five escapees crossed the many rivers by dragging each other over with a long pole. The procedure consumed so much energy that they decided another man had to die. This time it was Thomas Bodenham's turn. Greenhill split his skull with an axe and the remaining four men ate him until there was nothing left.

They had been on the run for nearly a month when John Mather fell seriously ill with dysentery. Aware that he was next for the axe, he begged to be allowed to pray before they killed him. He then 'laid down his head and Greenhill took the axe and killed him'.

Shortly after Mather had been eaten, Matthew Travers was bitten by a snake. As he weakened, he, too, was axed to death.

Now, there were only Pearce and Greenhill left. Greenhill had the sole axe, which he zealously guarded. Neither man dared to sleep, for fear that he would be killed by the other.

After several days of playing a deadly game of cat and mouse, both men were exhausted. Against his better judgement, Greenhill fell asleep.

Pearce seized the opportunity. 'I run up [sic], and took the axe from under his head, and struck him with it and killed him.' He hacked off Greenhill's arm and thigh and took them with him.

Pearce continued through the wilderness for several days until he reached a clearing that was being farmed by a shepherd. The shepherd took pity on Pearce and offered him shelter. Once he was restored to health, Pearce fell in with a couple of criminal bushrangers and lived with them for two months before all three men were tracked down and captured. By this time, Pearce had been on the run for four months, of which almost half had been spent in the wild.

Pearce was placed under lock and key in Hobart, where he made a full and frank confession to the Reverend Robert Knopwood, the town's chaplain and magistrate. Knopwood didn't believe Pearce's account of cannibalism – it was too horrific – and had him sent him back to Macquarie Harbour.

Within a few months Pearce once again made his escape, this time taking with him a young lad named Thomas Cox.

Cox's freedom was to prove short-lived. Pearce killed him within a few days and was in the process of eating him when he was once again captured. This time his tales of cannibalism were found to be true, for poor Cox's mutilated remains were discovered nearby.

Pearce was hanged in July 1824. Shortly before he died, he was heard to say: 'Man's flesh is delicious. It tastes far better than pork or fish.'

After his death, his body was given to a surgeon and dissected. His skull was eventually presented to the Academy of Natural Sciences in Philadelphia where it was given pride of place in a glass showcase.

It remains there to this day.

24

Edwin Darling's Nightmare

L ieutenant Colonel Edwin Darling was confident that he
ran the most secure prisoner-of-war camp in Britain.

Camp 198 near Bridgend in South Wales, known
locally as Island Farm, was surrounded by a high-wire fence and
equipped with searchlights and guard dogs. At night, sentries
made frequent patrols around the site.

There was good reason for the security. By the spring of 1945,
the camp housed more than 2,000 German POWs. These included several elite SS commanders and half-a-dozen Luftwaffe
fighter pilots. When these hardened Nazis had been brought to
the camp, they arrived in defiant mood, singing 'we are marching to England'.

Darling knew that any successful escape would be a propaganda disaster. The last thing he wanted was a German equiva-
lent of the Allied breakout from Stalag Luft III. The men involved
in that escape had been feted as heroes and their courage would
later be immortalized in the Hollywood movie *The Great Escape*.

On the evening of 10 March 1945, Darling retired to bed

unaware of anything untoward in the offing. The evening roll call had brought no unwelcome surprises and the prisoners had returned to their dormitories without trouble.

The only clue that something was wrong came later that night, when Darling's sleep was interrupted by the sound of prisoners singing loudly. But this was not unusual, for the inmates of Camp 198 often sang until late into the night.

Their rousing choruses were for a purpose. For many months, they had been secretly digging a huge underground tunnel that led from Hut 9 to the outside world. By the second week of March, it was complete and scores of prisoners were hoping to make their escape.

The 70-foot tunnel was a consummate work of German engineering. It descended deep into the clay subsoil before rising towards a small opening in a newly ploughed field on the far side of the perimeter fence. The prisoners had excavated it using knives and cooking utensils stolen from the camp kitchens.

The soil was disposed of in novel fashion. The POWs had managed to construct a fake wall at the end of Hut 9, using old tiles and bricks. They then pushed the excavated soil through a false air vent and into the cavity behind the wall.

The tunnel's roof was supported with wood stolen from oak benches in the canteen and the floor was lined with old clothes to ensure that escapees would not get dirty. There was even electric lighting, which could be used as a warning system whenever a guard was approaching.

Most extraordinary of all was the tunnel's air supply. Dozens of milk tins had been linked together to form a tube and air was forced through this tube by means of a four-bladed fan.

The night of the great escape was meticulously planned. Each prisoner was given an allotted time to pass through the tunnel and many of the men were equipped with maps of the local area. Some planned to steal cars and drive to Cardiff in the hope of smuggling themselves aboard ships heading to the continent. Others, emboldened by their training as pilots, hoped to steal planes and fly back to Germany.

It was shortly before midnight when the great escape began. Among the escapees was an SS officer named Karl Ludwig and his colleague Heinz Herzler. They slipped through the tunnel and successfully emerged into the field beyond the perimeter fence. They then followed their fellow escapees into the surrounding woodland.

As they crept along the road towards Cardiff, they encountered a drunken man returning home. They hid themselves in a hedge and waited for him to pass.

It was an unfortunate hiding place. The man staggered over to where Karl Ludwig was crouched in the undergrowth and answered a call of nature, unaware that he was urinating on an SS officer.

Most escapees had chosen to flee from the camp in small groups. One band of four men made their getaway in a stolen car. Others went on foot, trying to reach nearby railway stations before dawn.

Back at Camp 198, Lieutenant Colonel Darling slept on through the night, ignorant of what was taking place. It was not until 2.15 a.m., four hours after the first batch of prisoners had escaped, that the camp guards heard strange noises and realized something was wrong. They immediately awoke Darling and then raised the alarm. A rollcall of prisoners revealed that almost ninety had gone missing.

By daybreak, a massive nationwide manhunt was under way. According to the *Daily Express*, 'spotter planes flew over the Vale of Glamorgan while troops, Home Guard and police, all armed with tommy guns, searched the woods, fields and ditches'.

Though well trained, the German prisoners were at a huge disadvantage. They were highly conspicuous and poorly equipped. Karl Ludwig and Heinz Herzler redoubled their efforts to reach Cardiff after their unfortunate incident in the hedge, but it was not long before they were sighted by a local policeman named Philip Baverstock. He promptly arrested them.

Other prisoners were even less successful: most were captured within a few miles of the camp and it was not long before all of them were soon back in their huts.

At least that was the official version of the story. But how many really escaped? And how many were recaptured?

Unofficial accounts suggest that 84 prisoners got out of the camp, 8 more than the Allied POWs who escaped from Stalag Luft III. But because 14 were quickly recaptured, officials claimed (for propaganda purposes) that only 70 Germans escaped.

When the issue was raised in parliament, the Minister of War, Arthur Henderson, assured the country that the actual number was 67. There was good reason for him being economical with the truth. Several days after the breakout, three suspicious-looking Germans – escaped prisoners – were spotted near Canterbury in Kent. They managed to evade capture and were never seen again.

What happened to them remains a mystery. The most likely explanation is that they stole a boat and tried to make it back to Germany. Whether or not they were successful remains unclear.

But their empty beds at Camp 198 must have been a thorn in the side of Edwin Darling and a constant reminder that he had presided over one of the greatest prison breakouts of the Second World War.

PART IX

A Painful End

Hosoya did not want the case to arouse the other judges sexually if they might then discover that their wives were having their periods, since they would be without the proper means of relieving their excitement.

KEIJIRO HOSOYA, SENIOR JUDGE IN THE SADA ABE CASE,
EXPRESSES HIS CONCERN THAT HIS FELLOW JUDGES WILL
BE SEXUALLY AROUSED BY THE EROTIC DETAILS.

25

Never Go to Bed with a Knife

I t was the most sensational trial in years – one so sexually charged that even the judge confessed to being aroused by the evidence.

In the dock stood Sada Abe, one-time geisha, prostitute and waitress who was accused of strangling her lover in an elaborate sex game. That was not all. Once he was dead she had cut off his penis and testicles with a large kitchen knife and kept them as a sex toy.

There was never any doubt as to her guilt: Abe freely admitted to what she had done. What made the case so compelling was her graphic testimony. The sexual practices in which she indulged were so dark and dangerous that they sent shockwaves through the conservative Japanese society of the 1930s. Yet they were also to turn Sada Abe into a national celebrity, with her exploits feted in scores of books and half-a-dozen films. Even today, Sada Abe has the status of a bizarre icon.

Abe's sexual life had begun brutally at the age of fifteen when she was raped by a family acquaintance. Her father subsequently sold her to a geisha house, justifying his actions by saying it would bring structure to her life. But Abe proved an unwilling student. Before long she had turned to street prostitution, working in Osaka's brothel district.

In 1936, she had a dramatic change of lifestyle, getting herself a job in a Tokyo restaurant owned by a gregarious individual named Kichizo Ishida. The forty-two-year-old Ishida was married, but this had not stopped him from having a string of extramarital affairs. In Sada Abe, he found a partner who was willing to experiment with dangerous sexual practices.

Abe grew increasingly fixated with Ishida, but she also became obsessively jealous of his wife. She wanted to have Ishida all to herself and possess him, but he refused to leave the family home.

One evening, Abe went to the theatre and watched a play in which a geisha threatened her lover with a knife. Enthralled by what she saw, she bought herself a large kitchen knife and suggested to Ishida that it could be an instrument for sexual pleasure.

Most men would have made their excuses and left, but not Ishida. He was aroused by her threats and agreed that the knife could add an interesting twist to their extreme lovemaking. The two of them headed to the red-light district in the Ogu neighbourhood where they rented a room.

Every last detail of that fateful night was recounted by Sada Abe at her trial. She told the judge how she had put the kitchen knife to the base of Ishida's penis and said that she would make sure he'd never play around with another woman. Ishida assumed she was joking and got a perverse kick out of the threat.

After forty-eight hours of sustained lovemaking, Sada Abe began a whole new sex game. She removed the sash from her kimono and wound it tightly around Ishida's neck. It was the first time he had experienced erotic asphyxia and found that it heightened his sexual pleasure.

Sada asked him to do the same to her. She, too, found it exhilarating. They repeated the process for more than two hours, until Ishida's face became so distorted that it would not return to its normal appearance. He took thirty tablets of the sedative Calmotin to soothe the pain.

At around 2 a.m. on the morning of 18 May, as Ishida slept, Abe wrapped her sash twice around his neck and strangled him to death. She later told police: 'After I had killed Ishida I felt totally at ease, as though a heavy burden had been lifted from my shoulders, and I felt a sense of clarity.'

After lying with his corpse for several hours, she severed his genitalia with the kitchen knife and wrapped them in a magazine cover. She used his blood to write *Sada, Kichi Futari-kiri* ('Sada, Kichi together') on his left thigh and also on the bed sheet. She then put on his underwear and left the inn at about 8 a.m.

Ishida's mutilated corpse caused a sensation when it was found. Sada Abe was the obvious culprit, but she had disappeared without trace. A nationwide hunt failed to find her, even though she did nothing to hide her whereabouts. She stayed in a Toyko inn, had a massage and went to various bars.

Her behaviour, already disturbingly bizarre, now took an even darker turn. In the privacy of her hotel room, she started to engage in necrophilia. 'I felt attached to Ishida's penis and thought that only after taking leave from it quietly could I then die. I unwrapped the paper holding them and gazed at his penis and scrotum. I put his penis in my mouth and even tried to insert it inside me. It didn't work however, though I kept trying and trying.'

Two days after the murder, the police eventually tracked Abe down to her hotel room. She gave herself up immediately. 'Don't be so formal,' she said to the police. 'You're looking for Sada Abe, right? Well that's me. I am Sada Abe.' The police were still not convinced, so she showed them Ishida's genitalia.

The interrogating officer was struck by Abe's demeanour when asked why she had killed Ishida. 'Immediately she became excited and her eyes sparkled in a strange way.'

Her answer was: 'I loved him so much. I wanted him all to myself. But since we were not husband and wife, as long as he lived he could be embraced by other women. I knew that if I killed him no other woman could ever touch him again, so I killed him.'

On 21 December 1936, Sada Abe was convicted of murder and the mutilation of a corpse. She was sentenced to just six years in prison – an extremely lenient sentence for murder – yet she didn't even serve the full term. On 10 November 1940, her sentence was commuted and she was released. Despite her horrific crime, she was allowed to walk free.

In the years that followed, she was often asked why she had severed Ishida's penis. Her answer was logical if bizarre. 'I wanted to take the part of him that brought back to me the most vivid memories,' she said.

For a while she cashed in on her notoriety, but eventually she tired of the publicity and disappeared from the public eye. Her last years are believed to have been spent in a Kansai nunnery.

As for Ishida, his penis and testicles were moved to the pathology museum at Tokyo University's Medical School. They remained on public display for some years until they mysteriously disappeared. No one has subsequently been able to trace their whereabouts.

Further Reading

1. When Lenin Lost His Brain

Gregory, Paul R., *Lenin's Brain and Other Tales from the Secret Soviet Archives* (Hoover Institution Press Publication, 2008).

Kreutzberg, G.W., Klatzo, I., Kleihues, P., Oskar and Cécile Vogt, 'Lenin's Brain and the Bumble-bees of the Black Forest' (*Brain Pathology*, October 1992, Volume 4).

Zbarski, I.B., Samuel Hutchinson, *Lenin's Embalmers* (The Harvill Press, 1998).

2. Into the Monkey House

Adams, Rachel, *Sideshow USA: Freaks and the American Cultural Imagination* (University of Chicago Press, 2001).

Verner, Phillips, Blume, Harvey, *Ota Benga: The Pygmy in the Zoo, One Man's Degradation in Turn of the Century America* (Schwartz Publishing, 1993).

3. The Human Freak Show

Crais, Clifton, Scully, Pamela, *Sara Baartman and the Hottentot Venus: A Ghost Story and a Biography* (Princetown University Press, 2010).

Holmes, Rachel, *The Hottentot Venus: The Life and Death of Saartjie Baartman: Born 1789 – Buried 2002* (Bloomsbury, 2008).

Qureshi, Sadiah, 'Displaying Sara Baartman, the Hottentot Venus' (*History of Science*, 2004, Issue 42).

Further Reading

4. Freak Wave

Dash, Mike, *The Vanishing Lighthousemen of Eilean Mór* (Fortean Studies, 1998).

McCloskey, Keith, *The Lighthouse: The Mystery of the Eilean Mor Lighthouse Keepers* (The History Press, 2014).

Northern Lighthouse Board, 'The Mystery of Flannan Isle' (http://www.nlb.org.uk/historical/flannans.htm).

5: Japan's Deadly Balloon Bomb

Anon, 'Saw Wife and Five Children Killed by Jap Balloon Bomb' (*Seattle Times*, 1 June 1945). Available online: http://web.archive.org/web/20140417180525/http://www.stelzriede.com/ms/html/sub/mshwfug2.htm).

Mikesh, Robert C., *Japan's World War II Balloon Bomb Attacks on North America* (Smithsonian Institution Scholarly Press, 1990).

Powles, James, M., 'Silent Destructions: Japanese Balloon Bombs' (*World War II*, 2003, Vol. 17).

6. Never Go to Sea

Miskolcze, Robin, *Women and Children First* (University of Nebraska Press, 2008)

Saunders, Ann, *A Narrative of the Shipwreck and Sufferings of Miss Ann Saunders* (1827)

7. Eiffel's Rival

Barker, Felix and Hyde, Ralph, *London as it Might Have Been* (John Murray, 1995).

Hodgkins, David, *The Second Railway King: The Life and Times of Sir Edward Watkin, 1819–1901* (Merton Priory Press, 2002).

Lynde, Fred. C., *Descriptive Illustrated Catalogue of the Sixty-Eight Competitive Designs for the Great Tower for London* (The Tower Company, 1890).

8. Emperor of the United States

Cowen, Robert Ernest, 'Norton I, Emperor of the United States and Protector of Mexico' (San Francisco California Historical Society 1923, http://www.emperornorton.net/NortonI-Cowan.html).

Drury, William, *Norton I, Emperor of the United States* (Dodd, Mead, 1986).

Lane, Stanley Allen, *Emperor Norton: Mad Monarch of America* (Cadwell Caxton, 1939).

Further Reading

9. The Man Who Bought His Wife

Brander, Michael, *The Perfect Victorian Hero: The Life and Times of Sir Samuel White Baker* (Mainstream, 1982).

Shipman, Pat, *To the Heart of the Nile: Lady Florence Baker and the Exploration of Central Africa* (HarperCollins, 2004).

10. Hitler's Final Hours

Fest, Joachim, *Inside Hitler's Bunker: The Last Days of the Third Reich* (Farrar, Straus and Giroux, 2004).

Junge, Traudl and Muller, Melissa, *Until the Final Hour: Hitler's Last Secretary* (Weidenfeld and Nicolson, 2003).

Trevor-Roper, Hugh, *Last Days of Hitler* (Macmillan, 1995).

11. Seizing Eichmann

Aharoni, Zvi and Dietl, Wilhelm, *Operation Eichmann: The Truth About the Pursuit, Capture and Trial* (Wiley, 1997).

Harel, Isser, *The House on Garibaldi Street: The First Full Account of the Capture of Adolf Eichmann* (Viking, 1995).

Pearlman, Moshe, *The Capture of Adolf Eichmann* (Weidenfeld and Nicolson, 1961).

12. The Celebrity Executioner

Klein, Leonora, *A Very English Hangman: The Life and Times of Albert Pierrepoint* (Corvo Books, 2006).

Pierrepoint, Albert, *Executioner: Pierrepoint* (Harrap, 1974).

13. Trapped on an Iceberg

Grenfell, Wilfred, *Adrift on an Ice-Pan* (Houghton Mifflin, 1909).

Reason, J., *Deep Sea Doctor* (Edinburgh House Press, 1941).

14. Volcano of Death

San Diego State University Department of Geological Science, 'How Volcanoes Work: Mt Pelée Eruption (1902)'. Available online: http://www.geology.sdsu .edu/how_volcanoes_work/Pelee.html.

Scarth, Alwyn, *La Catastrophe: The Eruption of Mount Pelée, the Worst Volcanic Disaster of the 20th Century* (Oxford University Press, 2002).

Zebrowski, Ernest, *The Last Days of St. Pierre: The Volcanic Disaster that Claimed 30,000 Lives* (Rutgers University Press, 2002).

15. The Female Robinson Crusoe
McClanahan, Alexandra, 'The Heroine of Wrangel Island', (http://www.litsite .org/index.cfm?section=History%20and%20Culture&page=Life%20in%20 Alaska&ContentId=850&viewpost=2).
Niven, Jennifer, *Ada Blackjack: A True Story of Survival in the Arctic* (Hyperion, 2003).

16. The Last Post
Perisco, Joseph, *Eleventh Month, Eleventh Day, Eleventh Hour* (Arrow Books, 2005).
Rodricks, Dan, 'The Sad, Senseless End of Henry Gunther' (*Baltimore Sun*, 2008).

17. To Hell and Back
Graham, Don, *No Name on the Bullet* (Viking Press, 1989).
Murphy, Audie, *To Hell and Back* (St Martin's Press, 2002).
Official website: 'Audie L. Murphy Memorial Website' (http://www.audiemurphy .com).

18. Let's Talk Gibberish
McClain, Sally, *Navajo Weapon: The Navajo Code Talkers* (Rio Nuevo Publishers, 2002).
Tso, Samuel, 'Code Talker Samuel Tso: Navajo Oral History Project' (Navajo People, Culture and History: http://navajopeople.org/blog/code-talker-samuel -tso-navajo-oral-history-project/).

19. Good Ship *Zong*
Krikler, Jeremy, 'The Zong and the Lord Chief Justice' (*History Workshop Journal*, 2007, Vol. 64).
Walvin, James, *The Zong: A Massacre, the Law and the End of Slavery* (Yale, 2011).
Weisbord, Robert, 'The Case of the Slave-ship Zong, 1783' (*History Today*, 1969, Vol. 19).

Further Reading

20. The Suspicions of Inspector Dew

Connell, Nicholas, *Walter Dew: The Man Who Caught Crippen* (The History Press, 2012).

Goodman, Jonathan, *The Crippen File* (Allison & Busby, 1985).

Saward, Joe, *The Man Who Caught Crippen* (Morienval Press, 2010).

21. Dead as a Dodo

Hume, Julian, Martill, David & Dewdney, Christopher, 'Palaeobiology: Dutch Diaries and the Demise of the Dodo' (*Nature*, 2004, Vol. 429).

Roberts, David L., & Solow, Andrew R., 'Flightless birds: When did the Dodo become Extinct?' (*Nature*, 2003, Vol. 426).

22. A Sting in the Tale

Forbes, Rosita, *The Sultan of the Mountains: The Life Story of Raisuli* (Henry Holt and Company, 1924).

Harris, Walter, *Morocco That Was* (William Blackwood & Sons, 1921).

Harris, Walter, *The Land of the African Sultan: Travels in Morocco* (Sampson Low, Marston, 1889).

23. And Then There Were None

Collins, Paul, *Hell's Gates: The Terrible Journey of Alexander Pearce, Van Diemen's Land Cannibal* (South Yarra, 2002).

Sprod, Dan, *Alexander Pearce of Macquarie Harbour* (Cat & Fiddle Press, 1977).

24. Edwin Darling's Nightmare

Island Farm Websites: 'Island Farm Prisoner of War Camp: 198' (http://www.islandfarm.fsnet.co.uk) and 'Welcome to Island Farm' (http://www.bracklaordnance.co.uk/island%20farm.htm)

Philips, Peter, *The Great German Escape* (Seren, 2005).

Williams, Herbert, *Come Out, Wherever You Are: The Great Escape in Wales* (Gomert Press, 2004).

25. Never Go to Bed with a Knife

Johnston, William, *Geisha, Harlot, Strangler, Star: A Woman, Sex, and Morality in Modern Japan* (Columbia University Press, 2005).

Schreiber, Mark, *The Dark Side: Infamous Japanese Crimes and Criminals* (Kodansha, 2001).